How To Make The Most Of Every Audit:
An Etiquette Handbook For Auditing

D1117866

Also available from Quality Press

Quality Audits for Improved Performance
Dennis R. Arter

The Quality Audit: A Management Evaluation Tool
Charles A. Mills

Management Audits: The Assessment of Quality Management Systems, Second Edition
Allan J. Sayle

Auditing a Quality System for the Defense Industry
Charles B. Robinson

How to Plan an Audit
ASQC Quality Audit Technical Committee; Charles B. Robinson, editor

Audit Standards: A Comparative Analysis
Walter Willborn and the ASQC Quality Audit Technical Committee

ANSI/ASQC Q1-1986 Generic Guidelines for Auditing of Quality Systems

To request a complimentary 80-page catalog of publications, call 800-952-6587

How To Make The Most Of Every Audit:
An Etiquette Handbook For Auditing

Charles B. Robinson

ASQC Quality Press
Milwaukee, Wisconsin

How To Make The Most Of Every Audit:
An Etiquette Handbook For Auditing
Charles B. Robinson

Library of Congress Cataloging-in-Publication Data

Robinson, Charles B.
    How to make the most of every audit: an etiquette handbook for auditing/Charles B. Robinson.
        p.   cm.
    Includes bibliographical references and index.
    ISBN 0-87389-158-9
    1. Quality control — Auditing. I. Title.
TS156.R622 1992
658.5'62 — dc20

92-989
CIP

10 9 8 7 6 5 4 3 2 1

ISBN 0-87389-158-9

Acquisitions Editor: Jeanine L. Lau
Production Editor: Mary Beth Nilles
Marketing Administrator: Susan Westergard
Set in Garamond Book Condensed by Zahn-Klicka-Hill. Cover design by Laura Bober.
Printed and bound by BookCrafters.

For a free copy of the ASQC Quality Press Publications Catalog, including ASQC membership information, call 800-952-6587.

Printed in the United States of America

Printed on recycled paper

ASQC
Quality Press
611 East Wisconsin Avenue
Milwaukee, Wisconsin 53202

CONTENTS

PREFACE

The quality profession is often looked upon as a necessary evil that doesn't produce or ship a product to the customer. Management with this view believes that their quality personnel are expendable because they are not part of a "value added" function. When a layoff occurs, those within the quality organization are the first to go.

Management fails to realize that the quality professional is highly skilled both technically and behaviorally and is vital to the health of any organization. As with the quality professional, the medical professional does not produce or ship a product, but assists in maintaining and improving health.

To help people understand the value of the quality profession, this book makes the correlation between the quality world and the medical world. Both professions are needed even though at times they are the cause of pain and embarrassment. The role of the quality (medical) professional is vital, both when a company (person) is on a quality (health) maintenance program and when its quality (health) is on a downswing.

We make a living by what we get,
we make a life by what we give.

Additionally this analogy of our physical health to a company's quality health crosses all international borders; it is applicable worldwide. The International Standards Organization (ISO) 9000 series (or ANSI/ASQC Q90 series) documents are tangible evidence that quality is international in scope. The majority of the industrialized world has adopted or is making plans to adopt these documents as an international standard for quality systems.

The quality professional constantly evaluates organizations, products, services, statistical data, contract/project requirements, and so on. Whatever title there is within the quality organization (vice president, director, manager, project engineer, metrologist, test technician, inspection planner, or inspector), there is the need to evaluate, initiate, and/or become the catalyst that initiates improvement efforts. Because of this common denominator, this book is focused on quality auditing. Application of these principles, however, relates to every aspect of quality.

As international trade expands, our world will become smaller and the need for quality professionals will become more evident. This book will help people gain a new appreciation for the vital role that a quality professional has in our world. Quality is without international boundaries.

CHAPTER 1

A PROFESSIONAL
SOCIETY

GOVERNING SOCIETY

The American Medical Association (AMA) was formed in 1847 to aid "in the development of standards for the improvement of medical care." Similarly the American Society for Quality Control (ASQC) was formed in 1946 to be the leader in developing, promoting, advancing, and applying quality through a worldwide network of professionals.

As with the AMA, ASQC recognizes specific expertise within the profession. ASQC recognized such a field in 1979 and formed the Quality Audit Technical Committee (QATC). One of the goals of the QATC is to develop information and training material for those engaged in the audit/survey profession. The committee's membership is comprised of professionals representing a cross-section of industry: personal hygiene, pharmaceutical, nuclear power, consulting, aerospace, ship building, diesel engines, paper products, and so on.

The QATC is dedicated to providing industry with a common standard for auditors that will be universally recognized. To that end, it developed a Certified Quality Auditor (CQA) program similar to the Certified Quality Engineer (CQE). The CQA exam and an industry-recognized bibliography were approved by ASQC at the end of 1988.

ASQC has also recognized the Certified Reliability Engineer (CRE) category with equal stature. The AMA also has general fields of discipline and specialties within each field. Within the world of quality the CQA, CQE, and CRE are the general fields with specialties within the metal working, electronics, pharmaceutical, plastics, and banking fields.

Caution: Just as a licensed physician is a strong indication of professionalism, so is a CQA, CQE, or CRE. It is not, however, a guarantee. This achievement is similar to the military's Qualified Products List (QPL) which attests to the fact that a company made a specific product that met all the requirements at one point in time. The continued acceptance can only be achieved by a continued dedication of that company to produce only an acceptable product.

PUBLICATIONS

Both the AMA and ASQC have regular publications and encourage practitioners to author books. These publication endeavors are designed to inform their members of current, new, and advanced developments within their profession.

CODE OF ETHICS

ASQC has a Code of Ethics that has many similarities with the Hippocratic oath (oath exacted of his students by Hippocrates). These are noted as follows:

- AMA "Teach them this art if they shall wish to learn it . . . by precept, lecture, and every other mode of instruction."

  ASQC "Will strive to increase the competence and prestige of the profession . . . endeavor to aid the professional development and advancement of those in my employ or under my supervision."

- AMA "With purity and with holiness I will pass my life and practice my art."

  ASQC "Will be honest and impartial, and will serve with devotion my employer, my clients and the public."

- AMA "Whatever, in connection with my professional practice, or not in connection with it, I see or hear, in the life of men, which ought not to be spoken of abroad, I will not divulge."

  ASQC "Will not disclose information concerning the business affairs or technical processes of any present or former employer or client without his consent."

- AMA "I will follow that system of regimen which, according to my ability and judgment, I consider for the benefit of my patients."

  ASQC "Will do whatever I can to promote the reliability and safety of all products that come within my jurisdiction."

- AMA "Abstain from whatever is deleterious and mischievous."

ASQC "Will not compete unfairly with others."

The Hippocratic oath and the Florence Nightingale Pledge (physician and support staff) define a common philosophy of an honorable, supportive, confidential, and loyal profession. This is also the philosophy for the management and support staff of any quality organization.

THE FLORENCE NIGHTINGALE PLEDGE

I solemnly pledge myself before God and in the presence of this assembly, to pass my life in purity and to *practice my profession faithfully*. I will *abstain from* whatever is *deleterious and mischievous,* and will not take or knowingly administer any harmful drug. I will do all in my power to *maintain and elevate the standard* of my profession, and will *hold in confidence* all personal matters committed to my keeping and all family affairs coming to my knowledge in the practice of my calling. With *loyalty* will I *endeavor to aid* the physician in his work, and *devote myself to the welfare* of those committed to my care.

AN INTERNATIONAL PROFESSION

With today's transportation and communications systems our world is becoming smaller and smaller. Just like our medical expertise is applicable and transferable worldwide so is our quality expertise. Two contemporary indications of this shrinking world are EC92, where several European nations will disband trade barriers, and the ISO, which, as part of its activity, has developed internationally recognized quality standards.

You will find some cultural differences within the quality and medical profession. However, their applications are basically the same anywhere in the world.

International Commitment

Those of you who think this is just another high visibility activity that in time will die out should consider the following examples of international commitment.

1970 –	ISO Committee on Certification was formed.
1976 –	ISO's TC176 Committee was formed to address specific equations of quality assurance and quality management. This committee has worldwide membership, approximately 91 countries.
March 1987 –	ISO asked ASQC to evaluate how it could be involved in the IDO Third Party Assessments.
June 19, 1987 –	The American National Standards Institute (ANSI) and the ASQC issued the ANSI/ASQC Q90, Q91, Q92, Q93, and Q94 standards. These five documents were issued to be compatible with the ISO 9000-9004 documents.
September 1987 –	ASQC/ANSI adopted the ISO 9000-9004 Standards as American National Standards. They are designated Q90 through Q94.
August 7, 1989 –	The U.S. Assistant Secretary of Defense (P&L) issued a letter identifying his intention to work toward adoption of the ISO 9000 series quality system requirements.
October 1989 –	Eighteen nations, the European Community (EC), and European Free Trade Association (EFTA), adopted the European Norms (EN) 29001, 29002, and 29003 (ISO 9001, 9002, and 9003) as standards to be used for quality system assessments and certifications.
October 28, 1989 –	The Aerospace Industry Association (AIA) established a project to work with the Department of Defense to develop a method of adopting the ISO standards.

November 13, 1989 — ASQC formulated an affiliate company, Registrar Accreditation Board, whose purpose is to become the internationally recognized accreditation authority for the United States.

1989 — The North American Treaty Organization (NATO) started to develop new Allied Quality Assurance Publications (AQAP) to be compatible with the ISO Standards.

International Involvement

International involvement is not passive. Table 1 shows a list of countries that have developed their own quality standards to be compatible with ISO. Companies' engagement in international trade will soon be required to have an internationally recognized and certified quality system. Today there are companies in the aerospace, automobile, and paper industries that have obtained ISO certification to maintain their international customers.

The list of countries in Table 1 is impressive, but not complete. Table 2 is a list of countries that are participating or communicating with the ISO activity. This list is much larger and eventually they, too, will have developed their own comparable standard.

Table 1: International Standards Organization (ISO)

Standards Body (Country)	Quality management & Q assurance standards: Guidelines for selection & use	Quality systems: Model for quality assurance in design/develop. production installation & servicing	Quality systems: Model for quality assurance in production & installation	Quality systems: Model for quality assurance in final inspection & test	Quality management & Q system elements: Guidelines
ISO	ISO 9000:1987	ISO 9001: 1987	ISO 9002: 1987	ISO 9003: 1987	ISO 9004: 1987
Australia	AS 3900	AS 3901	AS 3902	AS 3903	AS 3904
Austria	OE NORM-PREN 29000	OE NORM-PREN 29001	OE NORM-PREN 29002	OE NORM-PREN 29003	OE NORM-PREN 29004
Belgium	NBN X 50-002-1	NBN X 50-003	NBN X 50-004	NBN X 50-005	NBN X 50-002-2
Canada	CSA Z2990-86	CSA Z299.1-85	CSA Z299.2-85	CSA Z299.4-85	CSA Q420-87
China	GB/T 10300.1-88	GB/T 10300.2-88	GB/T 10300.3-88	GB/T 10300.4-88	GB/T 10300.5-88
Denmark	DS/EN 29000	DS/EN 29001	DS/EN 29002	DS/EN 29003	DS/EN 29004
Finland	SFS-ISO 9000	SFS-ISO 9001	SFS-ISO 9002	SFS-ISO 9003	SFS-ISO 9004
France	NF X 50-121	NF X 50-131	NF X 50-132	NF X 50-133	NF X 50-122
Germany FR	DIN ISO 9000	DIN ISO 9001	DIN ISO 9002	DIN ISO 9003	DIN ISO 9004
Germany DR	TGL 29 513/02	TGL 29 513/03	TGL 29 513/04	TGL 29 513/05	TGL 29 513/06
Hungary	MI 18990-1988	MI 18991-1988	MI 18992-1988	MI 18993-1988	MI 18994-1988
India	IS:10201 Part 2	IS:10201 Part 4	IS:10201 Part 5	IS:10201 Part 6	IS:10201 Part 3
Ireland	IS 300 Part 0/ ISO 9000	IS 300 Part 1/ ISO 9001	IS 300 Part 2/ ISO 9002	IS 300 Part 3/ ISO 9003	IS 300 Part 0/ ISO 9004
Italy	UNI/EN 29000-1987	UNI/EN 29001-1987	UNI/EN 29002-1987	UNI/EN 29003-1987	UNI/EN 29004-1987
Malaysia	–	MS 985/ ISO 9001-1987	MS 985/ ISO 9002-1987	MS 985/ ISO 9003-1987	–
Netherlands	NEN-ISO 9000	NEN-ISO 9001	NEN-ISO 9002	NEN-ISO 9003	–
New Zealand	NZS 5600 Part 1 - 1987	NZS 5601 - 1987	NZS 5602 - 1987	NZS 5603 - 1987	NZS 5604 Part 2 - 1987
Norway	NS-EN 29000: 1988	NS-EN 29001: 1988	NS-ISO 9002	NS-ISO 9003	–
South Africa	SABS 0157: Part 0	SABS 0157: Part 1	SABS 0157: Part II	SABS 0157: Part III	SABS 0157: Part IV
Spain	UNE 66 900	UNE 66 901	UNE 66 902	UNE 66 903	UNE 66 904
Sweden	SS-ISO 9000: 1988	SS-ISO 9001: 1988	SS-ISO 9002: 1988	SS-ISO 9003: 1988	SS-ISO 9004: 1988
Switzerland	SN-ISO 9000	SN-ISO 9001	SN-ISO 9002	SN-ISO 9003	SN-ISO 9004
Tunisia	NT 110.18-1987	NT 110.19-1987	NT 110.20-1987	NT 110.21-1987	NT 110.22-1987
United Kingdom	BS 5750:1987: Part 0: Section 0.1 ISO 9000/ EN 29000	BS5750-1987: Part 1: ISO 9001/ EN 29001	BS 5750:1987: Part 2: ISO/9002 EN 29002	BS 5750:1987: Part 3: ISO 9003/ EN 29003	BS 5750:1987: Part 0: Section 0.2 ISO 9004/ EN 29003
USA	ANSI/ASQC Q90	ANSI/ASQC Q91	ANSI/ASQC Q92	ANSI/ASQC Q93	ANSI/ASQC Q94
USSR	–	40.9001 - 88	40.9002 - 88	–	–
Yugoslavia	JUS A.K. 1.010	JUS A.K. 1.012	JUS A.K. 1.013	JUS A.K. 1.014	JUS A.K. 1.011
European Com.	EN 29000	EN 29001	EN 29002	EN 29003	EN 29004
NATO	AQAP 100	AQAP 110	AQAP 120	AQAP 130	AQAP 131

Table 2:   Countries with Interest in the ISO Quality Systems

Albania (DSMA)	India (BIS)	Poland (PKNMIJ)
Algeria (INAPI)	Indonesia (DSN)	Portugal (IPQ)
Argentina (IRAM)	Iran (COSQC)	Saudi Arabia (SASO)
Australia (SAA)	Iraq (COSQC)	Singapore (SISIR)
Austria (ON)	Ireland (NSAI)	South Africa (SABS)
Bangladesh (BSTI)	Israel (SII)	Spain (AENOR)
Belgium (IBN)	Italy (UNI)	Sri Lanka (SLSI)
Brazil (ABNT)	Ivory Coast (DENT)	Sudan (SSD)
Bulgaria (BDS)	Jamaica (JBS)	Sweden (SIS)
Canada (SCC)	Japan (JISC)	Switzerland (SNV)
Chile (INN)	Kenya (KEBS)	Syria (SASMO)
China (CSBTS)	Korea, Dem. (CSK)	Tanzania (TBS)
Colombia (ICONTEC)	Korea, Rep. (KBS)	Thailand (TISI)
Cuba (NC)	Malaysia (SIRIM)	Trinidad (TTBS)
Cyprus (CYS)	Mexico (DGN)	Tobago (TTBS)
Czechoslovakia (CSN)	Mongolia (MSSB)	Tunisia (INNORPI)
Denmark (DS)	Morocco (SNIMA)	Turkey (TSE)
Egypt (EOS)	Netherlands (NNI)	United Kingdom (BSI)
Ethiopia (ESA)	New Zealand (SANZ)	USA (ANSI)
Finland (SFS)	Nigeria (SON)	USSR (GOST)
France (AFNOR)	Norway (NSF)	Venezuela (COVENIN)
Germany FR (DIN)	Pakistan (PSI)	Viet Nam (TCVN)
Ghana (GSB)	Papua New Guinea (PNGS)	Yugoslavia (SZS)
Greece (ELOT)	Peru (ITINTEC)	
Hungary (MSZH)	Philippines (BPS)	

CHAPTER 2

THE
PROFESSIONAL

THE CORRECT PERSPECTIVE

Quality professionals are sometimes thought of as "Big Brother." Unfortunately some individuals help to foster this impression. Quality is a highly skilled profession both technically and behaviorally. All quality professionals should approach their responsibility with the mind-set of a caring physician, not a destroyer.

The Quality Professional

THE DESTROYER	OR	A CARING PHYSICIAN
Negative mind-set		Positive mind-set
Indifferent		Empathetic
Know you're bad		Hope you're healthy
Enjoy deficiencies		Sensitive to emotions
Already know everything		Continue their education
Enjoy inflicting pain/embarrassment		Try to reduce pain/embarrassment
Gossip		Maintain confidentiality
Arrogant		Polite
Subjective		Objective
Blind-side you		Discuss concerns

Depending on which column best describes your approach you will either be a winner or a loser; the choice is yours.

The winner is always part of the answer.
The loser is always part of the problem.

The winner always has a program.
The loser always has an excuse.

The winner says, "Let me do it for you."
The loser says, "That's not my job."

The winner sees an answer to every problem.
The loser sees a problem for every answer.

The winner sees a green near every sand trap.
The loser sees two or three sand traps for every green.

The winner says, "It may be difficult but it's possible."
The loser says, "It may be possible but it's too difficult."

Be a winner!

Medical Examinations

My employer requests and schedules me for a medical examination. The frequency is based on my previous examination results with the maximum time between examinations. The physician and those who assist are highly trained in evaluating my present physical condition. After the examination they not only know my present condition, but are able to project my future health.

I follow a specific procedure to prepare for the medical examination, and the medical staff follow a specially designed examination worksheet. The worksheet they use is followed; however, equally important is their personal knowledge, training, and experience which sometimes cause them to evaluate additional aspects of my health.

One week after the examination I am called in to the doctor's office and given the results. During that time I am not only told my present condition, but also areas that I need to improve and what may happen if I don't heed the doctor's advice.

I bring areas in question to the doctor's attention so that they will be evaluated more closely. An interesting phenomenon occurs each time I am subjected to a medical examination: Areas that I had not thought of are identified as real or potential health problems. Fortunately I listen carefully and attempt to make the necessary corrections.

Quality Audits

An auditor also needs training, experience, and a worksheet to examine an organization's health and identify areas that need improvement. Those who really care about the continued health of their organization should welcome a professionally staffed audit team regardless of how they perceive themselves.

Auditors and audits are like doctors conducting medical examinations: They are professionals who evaluate one's current condition, systematically and regularly, and identify areas that are acceptable and those that need improvement. This is done so that we are able to make adjustments that will help ensure our health.

The medical examinations my family and I have are analogous to supplier audits and internal company audits. They are both at times embarrassing and painful, but in order to maintain a company's quality of life they are necessary.

PREQUALIFICATIONS

As with the medical profession quality professionals/auditors should be chosen from those who are academically superior. Those who are average or below will not have the necessary knowledge to professionally support a company. Ten or twenty years ago the quality department was similar to doctors of the wild west; some were well-trained professionals while others were "quacks."

Pressure from the public and industry have forced an upsurge in professionalism. Our respective clients are more sophisticated today and demand top-rate people.

EDUCATION

Industry in the past asked the first available inspector to go out and perform an audit: "After all, it is just like inspecting parts." We have found that in order to perform a meaningful audit a person needs far more than the skills of an inspector.

Years ago the doctors and auditors were predominantly general practitioners. Today, in addition to their fundamental skills, many of them are now specialists. The industry and medical fields have seen significant technological advances forcing the general practitioner to have a special field of expertise as well.

CONTINUING EDUCATION

After all the years of education one would think that a doctor would know everything. As with industry, the medical field is constantly changing and, therefore, quality auditors and doctors need to keep up with the current technology. Those who don't gradually become liabilities rather than assets.

When the AMA was formed in 1847, surgeons didn't even dream of heart or kidney transplants and they didn't feel the need to sterilize surgical instruments or even wash their hands between surgeries. We all are thankful that they were committed to continuous improvement through education.

The advancements in the quality profession are not transmitted by osmosis; it takes a commitment to continuous education. A true professional needs to diligently strive to keep current. The following are some ways in which this is accomplished:

- Reading technical literature, case studies, research papers, and so on.
- Attending seminars, schools, and so on.
- Actively participating in professional organizations.
- Consulting with peers in an effort to learn and share information.

PERSONAL TRAITS

The quality profession is a service and support profession aimed at verifying and helping to maintain the health of industry. As with other service professions there are many contacts with individuals who were not previously known. This fact makes a positive first impression important to a person's success.

You can only make a first impression once.

Your appearance and demeanor are two factors that influence one's first impression. Most people will respect and listen more intently to a person who is respectful in his or her conversation and mannerisms and neat in appearance. One's opinion of another person's technical prowess diminishes rapidly when there is a personality conflict.

A study in California showed that the most common reason

patients changed doctors was not because of lack of competence, but because of the doctor's bedside manner. Patients were troubled by insensitivity to their needs or by lack of respect for their views; the doctors were cold or arrogant. Poor communication, rather than poor treatment, was the basis of their complaints. The study pointed to four critical lessons about the value of having doctors and patients talk to one another. They are equally applicable to those working in the quality profession.

Full Communication   Candid communication between patient and physician is indispensable for an accurate diagnosis. When a physician asks about medical history and current health, the patient identifies areas that have caused some concern.

Actions by quality professionals need to gain the respect and confidence of the customer, company, and supplier. Quality professionals need to be able to communicate freely with people to be able to assist them in maintaining and improving their health.

Patient Awareness   Doctors should make patients aware that a damaged body can often repair itself to a remarkable degree. A doctor should avoid surgery if at all possible.

The quality professional should identify methods of improvement (prescriptions/exercise) that will allow the patient to implement his or her own improvements. Surgery on or amputation of areas/functions/people should be recommended only when absolutely necessary.

Fear and Panic   Fear and panic can make any disease worse.

The quality professional cannot afford to intimidate people. People can camouflage problems rather than bring them to the quality professional's attention.

Reassurance   Giving the patient a positive attitude toward his or her ability to maintain or regain health is vital. It often becomes a self-fulfilling prophecy.

The quality professional needs to have and exemplify a positive attitude toward a person's ability to make improvements. The psychology of dealing with people does not work unless there is genuine and true interest in others. All else is mere trickery and will fail sooner or later.

A quality auditor needs the bedside manners of a doctor to help attain the cooperation and respect of the organization or supplier being audited.

I have met some doctors and quality auditors who thought more highly of themselves than they should have. They very well may have been more intelligent than I, but an arrogant person becomes very small in my eyes. Arrogance doesn't belong in either profession.

A person who thinks highly of himself
is most assuredly a poor judge of character.

INTERNSHIP

Prior to receiving a license from the state board of medical examiners, a physician takes the Hippocratic oath, passes numerous exams during formal education, serves an internship, and passes a state board examination. The license to practice medicine within the state of California is especially fitting to this analogy: It is given by The Board of *Medical Quality Assurance.*

There are some experience requirements for becoming an ASQC CQA. Auditors must have eight years of experience in one or more of the areas identified in the CQA *body of knowledge,* at least a high school education, and a commitment to ASQC's Code of Ethics.

Experience or internship is required so that a person will have some of the rough edges smoothed out. People need to experience the real world while they are still in a protected environment. This is a time in which we are able to apply our skills under the watchful eye of a professional. During this period we are also maturing, a very necessary process for a person fresh out of school; all too often people just out of school believe they are all-knowing and invincible.

EMPATHY

There is little difference between a quality audit and a physical examination. Both disrupt one's schedule, take preparation, cause some embarrassment, and are sometimes painful. It is important for the professional to appreciate the uncomfortable position of the auditee (patient). The best way to achieve this understanding is to have been audited (to have had a physical examination). When performing a quality audit you should try to remember your experiences and treat the auditee as you would have liked to have been treated.

A friend of mine used an interesting process to select the physician that was going to give him a medical examination. He knew he was going to have a proctoscopic examination so he wanted a physician who had also undergone this sometimes painful and embarrassing procedure. He wanted someone who could empathize with him.

C H A P T E R 3

VARIETY WITHIN
THE PROFESSION

THE BIOLOGICAL FAMILY

The physician in general practice takes care of the whole family. Let's talk about each type of family member shown in the chart in Figure 1.

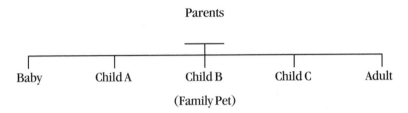

Figure 1: Biological Family

Parents Many have regular physical examinations because their health is important to the entire family.

Baby At birth babies get a physical examination to ascertain their health. While infants, they often see the doctor regularly. Good health during their formative years increases the probability of health throughout their lives.

Children Healthy children go to the doctor only when there is a health problem or when they want to participate in a sports program.

Adult Although they are mature and able to take care of their own medical needs, adults still have a constant relationship with their parents. My grown daughters occasionally ask my advice, just as I occasionally requested advice from my parents.

Family Pet I verified our pet's health when we first bought it. Now, other than regular shots, I only take the pet to the veterinarian when the need arises.

THE COMPANY FAMILY

The care of a biological family is similar to a company's family depicted in Figure 2. There is one major difference: The company family is "adopted." A company's family members were wanted and specifically chosen. There should be no "accidents" or "surprises."

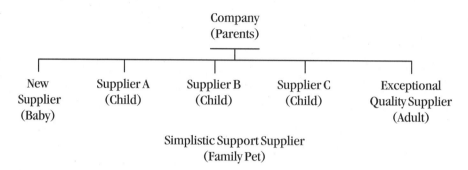

Figure 2: Company Family

Company A mature company knows the value of continuously improving its quality. It understands that continuous improvement is its fountain of youth and by continuously drinking from this fountain it will enjoy a long, vibrant life.

New Supplier At the "birth" of a new supplier, a company will examine its quality health and monitor it frequently to ensure childhood diseases are quickly identified and cured. Based on this intense care, the supplier has a higher probability of a long and healthy life.

Supplier An adolescent supplier increases monitoring and improving its own quality without customer intervention. Although its quality health is monitored, the frequency is adjusted based on performance. Those suppliers that want to add a special process are evaluated for their capability much like a child receives a special evaluation before participating in school sports.

Exceptional Quality Supplier There are those suppliers that virtually have a 100 percent quality rating and deliver their product or service on time, every time. These suppliers, although there is some contact with customers, have established a confidence level that significantly reduces the amount of customer evaluations.

Simplistic Support Supplier We all have a number of suppliers that provide a common service or product, the quality of which can be assessed at receipt. As with a pet, the company has a meaningful relationship with this supplier, although the supplier is not critical to the company's family. There may be an adjustment period, but another supplier with similar services or products can be found quickly.

SIZE OF COMPANY FAMILY

The number of physicians per 1,000 people is much lower in Third World countries. As a result there is less medical care and poorer health for the masses.

Yesterday we thought that using more suppliers was better because it increased competition. This can be equated to wanting more patients per doctor in an effort to drive the cost of medical care down; you end up with poor medical care. We need to reduce our supplier base so that we are able to support our chosen suppliers better.

Some companies have a great *fear* of reducing their supplier base; they are worried about competition and safety in numbers. They don't understand that this concern is often *false evidence appearing real (fear)*. Companies that are noted for their quality are successfully reducing their supplier bases in an effort to improve internal efficiency and work more closely with their suppliers.

Company	*Supplier Reduction*
Allen Bradley	20 percent in two years
Ford	45 percent in three years
3M	64 percent in three years
Motorola	70 percent in three years
Hewlett-Packard	47 percent in four months (one division)
Xerox	90 percent in one year

MOVING—NEW MANAGEMENT OR FACILITY

Several years ago I joined a company in Arizona. Before I was accepted for employment I was required to pass a medical examination. Shortly after I joined the company I developed an allergy to local vegetation which again drove me to see a doctor.

When a company changes facilities or there is a significant change in management it is often wise to perform a quality audit to assure their continued compliance to your requirements.

STARTING SPORTS—ADDING A NEW PROCESS

Before participating in a new sport it is wise to get a physical and to develop the flexibility and muscle tone required gradually.

A supplier wishing to start a new service or product should be audited to assure its capability of meeting the requirements without jeopardizing quality or delivery. You may have used the supplier successfully in the past, but when a new process is introduced you need the assurance that the supplier also has the necessary expertise in that new area.

ILLNESS—DEFICIENCIES

Known or suspected deficiencies must be resolved quickly. A successful company cannot let a deficiency go unchecked, regardless of how "insignificant" people may think it is.

Tumor—A Growing Concern

There are times when a supplier's products are acceptable, but other information about its performance causes the customer to be concerned. To alleviate the concern, an audit of that particular area is conducted.

This is similar to going to a doctor when we think we have a lump that previously wasn't there. We don't know if it's our imagination or a tumor, but we cannot afford to take any chances.

Cancer—A Known Problem

Suppliers with known problems that have an effect on the service or product they provide need to conduct the necessary investigation that will identify the cause or causes. Once identified, corrective action needs to be initiated immediately and then monitored.

Caught early enough, cancer may be cured either surgically or through treatments. If it is not caught early it is usually fatal.

CHAPTER 4

TOTAL HEALTH OF A COMPANY

The emergence of quality spokespersons like W. Edwards Deming, Philip B. Crosby, Genichi Taguchi, J.M. Juran, and A.V. Feigenbaum have made us aware that the quality of a company is the responsibility of everyone, not just the quality department. Companies that have this new mind-set are known as *total quality* or *world-class* companies.

Japan recognized that it needed companies of this stature to compete in the world market. Consequently, Japan established its Deming award several years ago in an effort to recognize world-class companies as well as to establish the criteria necessary to compete internationally. The United States recognized the value of this activity in the late 1980s and established the Malcolm Baldrige National Quality Award.

Only a select few companies are granted either of these awards. However, the self-assessment and preparation necessary to apply for the Malcolm Baldrige National Quality Award is beneficial, in and of itself. Some of the applicants also receive an independent and intense assessment by the awards organization. This independent evaluation can then be used to strengthen their quality systems and practices.

This chapter will look at the criteria used in the Malcolm Baldrige National Quality Award program. You will observe that the criteria involve much more than the quality organization; they assess the total quality of a company, both internally and externally.

The Malcolm Baldrige Award criteria are similar to a person's total well-being; it involves more than just his or her physical health. A professional tennis player is interested in more than muscle tone and coordination; the player's relationship with the sport and sporting world is also critical to his or her success. The player's popularity is enhanced when his or her physical health is balanced with interpersonal relationships with peers, news media, and the general public as well as with involvement in community affairs.

HEALTH MEASUREMENTS

During my annual physical I am evaluated on more than just what people see on the outside, that is, physical exercise, height and weight relationship, eating and drinking habits, and so on. The physician has a proven checklist that includes both a physiological (tangible and objective) and life-style evaluation. The life-style evaluation, though somewhat subjective, when compared with my physical condition provides an insight to my future health.

Similarly, the Malcolm Baldrige National Quality Award criteria has seven categories that encompass a company's total character. A company with a high score in one category is not sufficient; world-class companies need to excel in all areas. The maximum composite score is 1,000 points.

Table 3: 1991 Malcolm Baldrige National Quality Award Scoring System

Leadership — 100 points
    40 = Senior executive leadership
    15 = Quality values
    25 = Management for quality
    20 = Public responsibility

Information and Analysis — 70 points
    20 = Scope and management of quality data and information
    30 = Competitive comparisons and benchmarks
    20 = Analysis of quality data and information

Strategic Quality Planning — 60 points
    35 = Strategic quality planning process
    25 = Quality goals and plans

Human Resources Utilization — 150 points
    20 = Human resource management
    40 = Employee involvement
    40 = Quality education and training
    25 = Employee recognition and performance measurement
    25 = Employee well-being and morale

Table 3 continued on next page

Quality Assurance of Products and Services — 140 points
    35 = Design and introduction of quality products and services
    20 = Process and quality control
    20 = Continuous improvement of processes
    15 = Quality assessment
    10 = Documentation
    20 = Business process and support service quality
    20 = Supplier quality

Quality Results — 180 points
    90 = Quality of products and services
    50 = Business process, operational, and support service
    40 = Supplier quality results

Customer Satisfaction — 300 points
    30 = Determining customer requirements and expectations
    50 = Customer relationship management
    20 = Customer service standards
    15 = Commitment to customers
    25 = Complaint resolution for quality improvement
    20 = Determining customer satisfaction
    70 = Customer satisfaction results
    70 = Customer satisfaction comparison

Score Distribution

Leadership	100 points
Information/Analysis	70 points
Planning	60 points
Human Resources	150 points
Products and Services	140 points
Results	180 points
Customer Satisfaction	300 points

The score distribution vividly points out the importance of customer satisfaction; it is 316% more important than the results or actual quality of your product or service.

1991 MALCOLM BALDRIGE NATIONAL QUALITY AWARD: EXPLANATION OF THE SEVEN CATEGORIES

Leadership (100 points)

The leadership category examines how the senior executives create and sustain a clear and visible quality value system along with a supporting management system to guide all activities of the company toward quality excellence. Also examined are the senior executives' and the company's quality leadership in the external community and how the company integrates its public responsibilities with its quality values and practices.

Senior Executive Leadership (40 points)

> *Do not follow where the path may lead.*
> *Go instead where there is no path*
> *and leave a trail.*

The senior executives must have genuine leadership, personal involvement, and visibility in developing and maintaining an environment for quality excellence. You may see the senior executives on the production floor but that alone is not involvement. If the work force perceives their presence on the floor as "Big Brother," this communicates a negative involvement. The executives need to be on the floor so that they can appreciate the environment of the production workers as well as have the opportunity to get to know the people on a personal basis. If they are perceived to be part of the team, instead of the big boss, people will openly share their perspective of the manufacturing operation.

People at the executive level are given filtered information. This personal involvement will provide the executive with first-hand information that can be used to accurately evaluate the information formally presented to their office.

> *Smart is when you believe only half of what you hear.*
> *Brilliant is when you know which half to believe.*

Management by walking around (MBWA) will not provide a statistically based evaluation, but it does add value to the executive's insight.

26

Additionally it causes subordinates to be more candid in their reports; they know the boss has first-hand knowledge.

The value of this insight is best related to our everyday world. When you ask someone how they are doing they will normally say "great" or "couldn't be better." Those who know the respondents may tell you that their heart medicine just had to be increased or they just had to lay off a person due to the business forecast. If they were to answer your question honestly, they would say their life expectancy has been reduced or they are concerned about the future of a valued employee that they had to lay off. Human nature causes us to present as positive a picture as possible and all too often we don't bring enough realism into focus. Getting on the floor will help bring realism to the executive staff.

Quality Values (15 points)

Quality values are not limited to the values of those reporting to the quality department. This is an assessment of how a company's quality values are projected in a consistent manner, and how adoption of these values are assessed and reinforced throughout the company.

Let's check our quality values. A customer needs a product that, during inspection, is found to have a discrepancy. There is a dimension that is slightly out of tolerance; however, it has no effect on the fit, form, or function of the product, and will not be noticed by anyone. What is your response? Keep in mind that if you reject it you will not be able to ship it on time and the customer will be angry.

> *Watch your thoughts; they become words.*
> *Watch your words; they become actions.*
> *Watch your actions; they become habits.*
> *Watch your habits; they become character.*
> *Watch your character; it becomes your destiny.*
>
> *Frank Outlaw*

A company's mission statement needs to be heavily focused on quality. In the past, we focused on shipments that, in my opinion, had the cart before the horse; on-time shipments of poor quality, in the long run, are more detrimental than late shipments of high quality.

Quality values need to be identified in a companywide policy statement that everyone knows and is committed to.

*A company without quality values will
meet their values every time.*

Management for Quality (25 points)

Quality values alone are not enough; these values must be integrated into the day-to-day management of all units. It's nice to have top-level quality values that are published and known by all. It's quite another thing to implement these values throughout the organization.

If you have to constantly remind people of the company's quality policy then the quality policy isn't effective. The quality values need to be part of the company's "genetic code" that is operative without thought. Specific strategies need to be established.

Executive Strategies The executive management of a company needs to establish key strategies that are focused on improving quality in every department. The executives are the leaders and these strategies should have an effect on their own activity as well as the activity of all others. Published strategies need to be the focus of the work force and a topic during meetings, otherwise they aren't strategies, they are dreams. They need to set the tone so that the organization can follow.

Cooperative Strategies Management strategies must also address cooperation with others. Communication and teaming with various levels of management as well as with the supplier base need to be included in the strategies. It's an old saying, but, "Two heads are better than one."

Concurrent engineering is a valuable tool that should be included in a company's strategy. Here's an example.

A supplier was given a request for quote (RFQ) on a particular circuit board. The board was designed to meet the required performance characteristics. Unfortunately, the designer knew very little about the manufacturer's needs and didn't even consider the ease of manufacturing.

28

The supplier requested and obtained permission to propose another configuration. The revised design allowed the supplier to use commercially available modules and its own automatic component insertion equipment. The results were shorter lead time, more efficient and consistent manufacturing, and higher reliability—all at a lower cost while maintaining the desired performance characteristics.

Supportive Strategies   These strategies should also include a missionary spirit. When a department or supplier is having problems, the company should assist in bringing that area back to health. All too often we gather together not to help but to criticize.

Monitor the Effectiveness   All of these strategies are designed to improve the support of a company's customers. They do, however, need to be monitored. Monitoring the effectiveness of the strategies allows a company to fine-tune some strategies and identify those that are not effective. As a company becomes more dynamic so do its strategies and the company needs to be ready to change direction when required.

A significant side benefit to monitoring the effectiveness is to let management know that its improvement efforts are really working. Without management's involvement, people may lose interest and the effort will be replaced with things that "are visible to the boss."

When doctors identify an illness, they will often ask the patient to come back for a follow-up visit. This is to ensure that the medication is doing what they expected. The medical profession, like the quality profession, is not an exact science and should be monitored with corrections made when the needed results are not achieved.

Public Responsibility (20 points)

A company needs to extend its quality leadership to the external community. The public's health, safety, environmental protection, and ethical business practices are also part of a company's responsibility and need to be integrated into its quality policies and activities.

Community Awareness   A company needs to conduct itself as a responsible citizen. Its technical, employment, health, safety, environmental, and business talent should be shared. The following is a list of activities that company officials and employees could be involved in to better support their community:

- *Scouting.* Invite a scout troop to tour your facility.

- *City planning.* Be involved in the environmental issues within your community.

- *Schools.* Make yourself available to the schools in your area to talk about job opportunities or explain some of the technologies to science classes.

- *School boards.* Work with them to direct the education within high schools, trade schools, colleges, and universities to fit your business employment needs.

- *Local businesses.* Work with business leaders within the community to support local services and activities, i.e., parks, libraries, cultural events, and so on.

- *Charitable organizations.* Support community fund drives (Red Cross, United Way, and so on), blood banks, emergency response (natural disasters, fire departments, and so on) and other organizations that improve the community life.

- *Environment protection.* Internal and external responsibility regarding protection and improvement of the environment. Among the many areas to consider are careful control of manufacturing substances, employee car-pooling, and company landscaping.

- *Ethics.* Maintain awareness of ethics within the company and in dealing with the community government and business with which they deal.

Information and Analysis (70 points)

The information and analysis category examines the scope, validity, use, and management of data and information that underline the company's total quality management system. Also examined is the adequacy of the data and information to support a responsive prevention approach to quality based upon "management by fact."

Scope and Management of Quality Data and Information (20 points)

Data generation for data's sake is a waste of company resources. Management needs to be selective when identifying the data used to manage quality. The data need to be reliable, timely, and accessible to be useful in planning, managing, and evaluating quality.

The consistency and standardization of these data need to be clearly defined and enforced. This discipline is necessary if the data are to be used as a yardstick for measurement. This allows the company to compare data points over time, identifying weaknesses and strengths.

Some of the data elements a company should consider are as follows:

- Customer perception (consumer surveys, customer ratings, and so on)
- Employee development (training, recognition, and so on)
- Employee attitude
- Internal safety record
- Progress against benchmarks
- Internal Cpk's*
- Supplier Cpk's*
- Inventory turns

*See page 71 for explanation of Cpk.

Competitive Comparisons and Benchmarks (30 points)

The benchmarking process has been talked about in recent years. Few companies, however, have actually made a quality-related competitive comparison to a world-class operation. We have a tendency to talk about the inferiority of our competitors rather than look at areas in which they may outstrip our current practices.

Benchmarking starts internally with understanding and quantifying key areas within our own company that will be compared to industry leaders. Benchmarking leadership indicators should not be restricted to a specific industry; planning is done by all world-class companies and we should not restrict benchmarking to a select few.

Once you have completed the benchmarking and developed

31

action plans toward improvements, the process has just begun. Always be alert to new horizons of excellence that can be used to keep goals and targets focused on world-class performance. Even if a company reaches its target it has just begun the journey toward excellence.

Analysis of Quality Data and Information (20 points)

The above data are of little value unless the data and information are analyzed in a timely manner to support the company's key quality leadership objectives.

The use of these data transforms a company from one that has "continuous commitment toward improvement" to one that has "continuous measurable improvement." A commitment without measurements and goals is not visible enough to maintain support.

> *People will do what management inspects,*
> *not what management expects.*

This information must be current and reliable so that management can use it to effect real-time, long-range objectives. These measurements should support the following:

- Analysis of key systems
- Technological advancements
- Day-to-day quality improvement activity
- Policy development
- Human resource strategy development
- Cycle time reduction of information and products

Strategic Quality Planning (60 points)

The strategic quality planning category examines the company's planning process for retaining or achieving quality leadership and how the company integrates quality improvement planning into overall business planning. Also examined are the company's short-term and long-term priorities to achieve and/or sustain a quality leadership position.

Strategic Quality Planning Process (35 points)

The strategic quality planning process for a company's quality leader-ship and customer satisfaction must be both short-term (one to two years) and long-term (three to five years).

A strategic quality plan is key to a company's success. The plan needs to be realistically aggressive and should take the following areas and data into consideration:

- Competitive and benchmark data
- Customer requirements
- Supplier data
- Process capabilities
- Potential improvements in quality
- New technology
- Priority initiatives or projects
- Employee training improvements and needs

The goals or targets you set are often a prediction of things to come; they become self-fulfilling prophecies. Set your aim high.

The actual planning process needs to include input from a com-pany's supplier base, internal operation, and customers.

Quality Goals and Plans (25 points)

A company needs to document its principal quality priorities and plans, short-term (one to two years) and long-term (three to five years), that address the following:

- The company's leadership objectives
- Resource commitments toward education, training, and tech-nologic advancements
- Support of these objectives by their suppliers

*Those who don't have an objective
will meet it every time.*

Many of us are afraid to publish a milestone chart identifying principal quality priorities and plans as we don't want to be held accountable. This attitude is similar to those who tell themselves they will go on a diet and exercise program to lose weight. The less serious ones will not let their spouse know or measure their progress and soon will quit, just to start again another time. More often than not, the "tomorrow" attitude leads to continuous defects, not improvement.

Excellence can be attained if you:
- *Care more than others think is wise*
- *Risk more than others think is safe*
- *Dream more than others think is practical*
- *Expect more than others think is possible*

Human Resource Utilization (150 points)

The human resource utilization category examines the effectiveness of the company's efforts to develop and realize the full potential of the work force, including management, and to maintain an environment conducive to full participation, quality leadership, and personal and organizational growth.

Human Resource Management (20 points)

A company needs to recognize and plan for the involvement of its most valuable resource: people. They need to have strategies that involve customer/supplier partnerships, labor/management coopera-·tion, an employee recognition system, employee training, and educational initiatives.

All too often, we invest an inordinate amount of money into depreciating assets (capital equipment) to the neglect of our only appreciating asset (our employees). The return on investment may be less quantifiable but as a "Monday night quarterback" you will understand that it was the wisest investment.

Although I believe we need to invest in training, we must have a proper balance between the tools necessary to perform a task and the training and support of management.

For example, a construction supervisor wanted to improve the efficiency of house framing so he offered a trip to Hawaii to the person who could drive a nail with the greatest speed and efficiency. To one employee he gave all the training and management support known to mankind and to the other he gave a hammer.

Your human resource department should be aware of your company's mission statement and each department's objectives focused on supporting that statement. The human resource department often is responsible for training along with its other duties, and, therefore, needs to understand and plan for future training needs. It also needs to develop an organizational culture that encourages employees to improve their capabilities continuously. Once trained, individuals need to effectively employ those capabilities within their job responsibilities.

Those who improve their capabilities but cannot use them will soon forget what they learned. I took anatomy in school but today I can only remember that "the head bone's connected to the neck bone . . ." because I haven't had an opportunity to use that knowledge.

The human resource department needs to get involved with the operation. Its role is not to sit on the sidelines and give advice.

There's a big gap between advice and help.

Following are some of the planning strategies that should involve the human resource department:

- Measurements developed to monitor employee-related improvements at all levels and classifications: hourly, bargaining unit, contract, and management.

- Priorities, short- and long-term, that are focused on creating a culture of continuous improvement.

- Mechanisms for promoting cooperation such as internal customer/supplier techniques or other internal partnerships.

- Initiatives to promote labor-management cooperation such as partnerships with unions.

- Mechanisms for increasing or broadening employee responsibilities.

- Partnerships initiated with educational institutions to help develop employees and to ensure a future supply of well-prepared employees.

Employee Involvement (40 points)

Employees need to be involved in developing a company's quality objectives; concurrent engineering shouldn't be restricted to product-related activities. Actual employee involvement should be translated into a metric so that their continued involvement can be monitored and maintained.

I work for a multi-national company with more than 50,000 employees and $5.5 billion in sales. Within this large company we have a vast resource of knowledge and experience. To take advantage of these resources is a tall task, but one we know is worth our effort. The company employs nationally known experts in a variety of fields and many of these employees share their knowledge with other divisions.

A company needs to develop an organizational culture that enables, or empowers, employees to participate in planning, goal setting, problem solving, and decision making. A world-class company will have employees who:

- Act within the full scope of their job responsibilities.
- Interface with management beyond immediate supervision.
- Interface with customers when appropriate.
- Seek continuous improvements in creative ways.
- De-emphasize functional boundaries, allowing full exchange of information.

Quality Education and Training (40 points)

A company needs to decide what quality education and training is needed by their employees and how the employees will use the knowledge and skills acquired. The company should summarize the types of quality education and training provided in all departments, not just the quality department.

Companies need to encourage their employees to use the latest techniques and tools (see Chapter 6). Complementing this encouragement companies need to have the necessary training and support available so that people can also implement and perfect their use of these tools.

Those companies that cannot provide the training need to develop a form of recognition to those individuals who are motivated enough to obtain this knowledge from an outside source.

A good test to determine how serious management is toward training is to review the following data:

- Types of quality education and training given
- Quality orientation of new employees
- Percent of employees receiving training
- Cost of training per employee
- Yearly hours of quality education for each employee

Employee Recognition and Performance Measurement (25 points)

A company's recognition program should fall in line with Maslow's Hierarchy of Needs.*

1. *The physiological needs.* In the first place, the physiological needs are the most fundamental; they require satisfaction before other needs. Included in this group are the needs for food, water, air, rest, and so on that are required for maintaining the body in a state of equilibrium.

2. *The safety needs.* Once the physiological needs are satisfied, the individual becomes concerned over his or her physical and psychological well-being. These include the need for safety and security, both in a physical and psychological sense. The need to be protected from external dangers to our bodies and our personalities are included in this group. Most employees, for example, desire to work at jobs that are free from physical and psychological hazards, and that provide tenure.

3. *The belonging and love needs.* If both the physiological and the safety needs are fairly well satisfied, the belonging and love needs will emerge as dominant in a person's need structure. The need for attention and social activity are the major needs in this category. An individual desires affectionate relationships with people in general and desires to have a respected place in his or her group.

---

*A.H. Maslow is a psychologist who developed a theory of human motivation related to five human needs arranged according to priority.

At the top of the scale are the needs for esteem and self-realization. As the lower needs are satisfied, these higher needs become dominant. Very few of us ever fully realize the fulfillment of these higher needs.

4. *The esteem needs.* These include the desire for self-respect, strength, achievement, adequacy, mastery and competence, confidence in the face of the world, and independence and freedom. Also included in this group is the desire for reputation or prestige or respect and esteem from other people.

5. *The need for self-actualization (realization).* This refers to a person's desire for self-fulfillment; namely, to the tendency for a person to become actualized in what he or she potentially is. This tendency might be phrased as the desire to become more and more what one is, to become everything that one is capable of becoming.

Money is the motivator to some levels while public recognition is far more important to others. Employees who are recognized by management will continue to grow.

A plant without water will wither and die.

Metrics need to be developed for any recognition or award program. Without this visible and objective system the program can do more harm than good. These metrics need to accommodate both individual and group accomplishments toward improvement.

"The uninspected will inevitably deteriorate"; therefore, a company's recognition program needs to be constantly monitored to understand its contribution toward improved quality.

Employee feedback needs to be not only encouraged but solicited. Their input to a company's recognition program is key to its development and maintenance.

Employee Well-Being and Morale (25 points)

A company needs to safeguard the health and safety of employees, ensure comfort and physical protection, and maintain a supportive work environment. It also needs to summarize trends in employee well-being and morale.

The family aspect of a company should be evident to the casual observer. The total health of the employees needs to be a priority. A good test is to evaluate what your company is doing in the following areas:

- Quality improvement activities consider the well-being and morale factors such as health, safety, satisfaction, and ergonomics.

- Accidents and work-related health problems are investigated to determine the root cause and take the necessary corrective measures.

- Technology advancements and training are in concert so that employee development allows employee advancements.

- Employee clubs or other organized activities are sponsored by the company to meet some of the employees' social needs.

- Special services, facilities, and opportunities are made available by the company to support employees. These might include one or more of the following: counseling, assistance, recreation, culture, and non—work-related education.

Quality Assurance of Products and Services (140 points)

The quality assurance of products and services category examines the systematic approaches used by the company for total quality control of goods and services based primarily upon process design and control, including control of procured materials, parts, and services. Also examined is the integration of quality control with continuous quality improvement.

Design and Introduction of Quality Products and Services (35 points)

The design and introduction of new or improved products and services need to meet or exceed customer requirements. The processes need to be designed to consistently and reliably meet these requirements. This is demonstrated by the following:

- The effective use of cross-functional teamwork during product and service development.

- A complete definition of customer needs that includes product and service performance, quality, product costs, and delivery.

- The appropriate use of licensing or affiliation to obtain new technology.

- The adoption of simultaneous engineering methods, emphasizing progressive reduction of development time, and engineering changes during production.

- The use of such methods as group technology to optimize manufacturing costs and commonize product and process designs.

- The timely execution of design reviews that include such factors as manufacturing feasibility, measurement capability, and product safety.

- The use of such methods as failure modes and effects analyses to assure product, service, and process reliability.

- The regular use of design of experiments to optimize product performance.

- The active involvement with suppliers to assist in product development.

- A documented product release and sign-off system that involves all functional departments, suppliers, and customers as appropriate.

Process and Quality Control (20 points)

The processes that produce the company's products and services need to be controlled to yield quality results that meet design plans or specifications. There is an unfortunate saying in the ranks of top management: "Never mind the elegance of your golf swing; it's where you land the ball that counts."

This bias toward results over "process" has been the downfall of many businesses. Not controlling a process and inspecting the results is an emergency room procedure and the patients are sometimes transferred to the morgue.

Process planning and control is a cost-effective way to ensure compliance with requirements and to monitor ongoing improvements of process capabilities. The following activities are common in forward-thinking companies:

- Verify that the process instructions and control plans are adequate to ensure product conformance.

- Regularly use design of experiments to optimize process performance.

- Work with suppliers to assist them in problem solving, quality, and process improvement.

- Flowchart analyses of processes to identify key process operations and control points.

- Demonstrate that measurement accuracy and precision meet process and product requirements.

Continuous Improvement of Processes (20 points)

A company's products and services are not stagnant and need to be continuously improved through optimization and improvement of processes. A stagnant product or service is like a car going uphill without brakes. Without continuous improvement (forward advances) you will fall behind the competition (roll backward). There is no effort expended to roll backward; it's as effortless as falling off a cliff. World-class companies know that continuous improvement has a sense of urgency. They need to improve *quickly* and *now* to maintain and eventually to capture more of the market.

Improvements are made by people and their contribution toward the following:

- Analysis and optimization of each process

- Development of alternative processes

- Evaluation of new or improved technology

- Use of competitive and benchmark data

- Teaming with other departments to eliminate improvement roadblocks

The employees of a company must internalize this improvement initiative. Individual and collective improvements are necessary for a company's survival.

It is no use saying
"We are doing our best."
You have got to succeed in
doing what is necessary.

Winston Churchill

Quality Assessment (15 points)

A company needs to focus on meeting the customer's needs as well as the quality in its products, processes, services, and quality practices. Just as industry and technology are dynamic so are their procedures directing these activities.

Companies should have regularly scheduled evaluations to assess their quality systems and practices, and the quality of their products, processes, and services. The usefulness and integrity of the evaluation, perceived or real, is often influenced by who is conducting it. Additionally, the independence of the auditor and how frequently the evaluation is performed is also a factor.

The use of customer and government assessments are also used by a company to monitor the integrity of their internal system. This provides them with an unbiased assessment. The regular assessment of a company's operation and the involvement of upper management is critical to ensure a continued drive toward improvement.

The results of these evaluations should then be used as a management resource. Management can then provide the necessary resources to make improvements as well as monitor the improvement efforts through follow-up assessments.

The uninspected inevitably deteriorates.

Dwight D. Eisenhower

Documentation (10 points)

Documentation and other modes of knowledge preservation and transfer are important for a company to consistently support quality assurance, assessment, and improvement. A company that is consistent in its approach to total quality has documented procedures that are uniformly followed. Without this consistent base it is difficult to discover and correct systemic improvements.

Documentation must also be under some type of configuration management so that obsolete procedures and information are removed and replaced with current ones. Many companies are moving toward a paperless system and are computerizing their documentation which ensures that the documents/procedures are always current.

Statistical process control (SPC) is a tool that should not be restricted to the manufacturing floor; it can also be used to monitor and improve a company's documentation and procedures. Once the documented procedure is in place the applicable "process capability" can be monitored and the appropriate adjustments made.

As SPC limits are modified to keep up with technology so we need timely updates of documentation practices to keep pace with changes in technology, management, and quality improvements. The following is a list of areas/documentation that should be evaluated on a regular basis:

- Quality manuals
- Quality policy and procedures
- New employee orientation
- Training programs
- Process work instructions

The value of a company's documentation and procedures is measured in need and quality, not in quantity. Too much documentation is as harmful as too little. A company needs to be judicious in the creation of its internal documentation.

Procedures expand in proportion
to the resources available.

Business Process and Support Service Quality (20 points)

To be a leader, a company needs to keep quality in the forefront. As Ford Motor Company says, "Quality Is Job One"; this is applicable to everyone. There are departments outside of manufacturing and engineering that support a company's total quality effort. These support services (finance and accounting, management information services, maintenance, health, safety and environmental, research and development, sales, marketing, administration, human resources, legal council, and so on) should also be assured, assessed, and improved.

All of these activities should have plans for internal and third-party assessments that aid management in identifying improvement opportunities.

Supplier Quality (20 points)

A company is not self-reliant; its success or failure is greatly influenced by its suppliers. The quality of materials, components, and services furnished by other businesses is what a company uses to produce quality results; therefore, as its quality deteriorates, so does yours.

Keeping in mind that "you can't make a silk purse out of a sow's ear," it is imperative that a supplier's quality is assessed, assured, and improved, if possible. There are a number of ways to increase the confidence level in a supplier's quality; however, without personal involvement, management techniques will be shallow and short-lived. As a company matures, its methods of supplier evaluations will also mature to a point that the need for redundant inspections or audits will be significantly reduced. A sequence of maturity follows:

1. Receiving inspection

2. Source inspection

3. Variable inspection results monitored

4. Source-delegated inspection

5. SPC

6. Cpk's $\geq$ 1.33

7. Cpk's $\geq$ 2.0

A company cannot just sit back and wait for its suppliers to implement the necessary quality improvements. A company needs to assure the quality of the supplier's products or services by performing costly audits or inspections until the quality improvement efforts have been successful. During this maturing process, the company should be assisting the supplier through training, encouragement, council, and so on, just as parents train, encourage, and council their children during their maturing process.

It has been said that if you feed a man a fish, you've fed him once. If you teach him how to fish, you've fed him forever! Giving only occasional assistance to a supplier is the equivalent of feeding it once. Training the supplier is feeding the supplier forever.

Physicians don't identify an illness and then wait until the patient's health improves. They identify methods and provide resources to quicken the recovery cycle. Companies should also provide methods and offer training and assistance to ailing suppliers so that they can continually improve the quality of their processes.

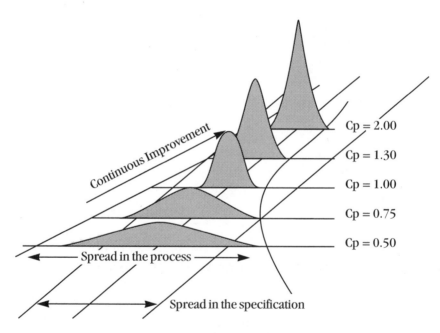

Figure 3: Continuous Process Improvement

Quality Results (180 points)

Contrary to an old saying, "It's the thought that counts," a company with good intentions isn't good enough. It needs to achieve high quality levels and fruitful quality improvement efforts. These measurements are based upon an objective analysis of customer requirements and expectations, business operations, and current quality levels in relation to those of competing firms.

*It isn't so much what we **talk about** and **know**,*
*but what we **practice** and **sow** that does the good.*

Today we express quality levels in a variety of ways: parts per million (PPM) defective, Cpk's, percent acceptable, and sigma (standard deviations). (See Table 4.)

Table 4: Quality Levels

PPM	Cpk	Percent	Sigma
133,600.0000	0.50	86.64	1.5
24,400.0000	0.75	97.56	2.25
2,700.0000	1.00	99.73	3.0
967.0000	1.10	99.9033	3.3
318.0000	1.20	99.9682	3.6
96.0000	1.30	99.9904	3.9
26.0000	1.40	99.9974	4.2
6.8000	1.50	99.99932	4.5
1.6000	1.60	99.99984	4.8
0.3400	1.70	99.999966	5.1
0.0600	1.80	99.999994	5.4
0.0018	2.00	99.99999982	6.0

Gone are the days when a company should be satisfied with a 99.73 percent quality level, either from their suppliers or internally. The competition understands the significant difference between a 3 sigma (99.73 percent) and a 6 sigma (100 percent) quality level. The following should help us better appreciate this difference:

- 2,700 PPM defective versus 0.0018 PPM defective
- 20,000 wrong drug prescriptions each year versus one wrong drug prescription in 25 years
- 15,000 newborn babies dropped by doctors and nurses yearly versus three newborn babies dropped in 100 years

- Unsafe drinking water almost one hour each month versus unsafe drinking water for one second every 16 years

- Two short/long landings at O'Hare airport each day (also New York, Los Angeles, Atlanta, and so on) versus one short/long landing in 10 years in all the U.S. airports

- Nearly 500 incorrect surgical operations per week versus one incorrect surgical operation in 20 years

- 2,000 lost articles of mail per hour versus 35 lost articles of mail per year

- No telephone service for nearly 10 minutes each week versus no telephone service for nearly six seconds in 100 years

- No television transmission for nearly 10 minutes each week versus no television transmission for nearly six seconds in 100 years

Quality of Products and Services (90 points)

The metrics used to assess a company's quality should not be limited to deliverable hardware or services. The metrics should be derived from customer needs and expectations related to a company's total operation. Areas to consider when developing these measurements are:

- Accuracy
- Timeliness
- Behavior
- Documentation
- After market service
- Reliability
- Performance
- Delivery
- Appearance

Using the measurements selected, a company will be able to summarize trends and outline what steps it needs to take to improve the customer's image.

Companies need to compare their current quality levels with

industry averages, industry leaders, and world leaders. A comparison of the key product and service quality measures reported in the previous category, quality of products and services, will identify both weak and strong areas.

Several industry associations publish industry statistics annually. The Aerospace Industry Association is one example. Yearly the AIA compiles 68 quality statistics from its association and publishes the results to its membership.

The medical world also releases standards for benchmarking. Although I usually don't like them, the new height and weight tables released in November 1990 were a pleasant surprise. It allows for a broader range of healthy weights than the 1985 guidelines – as much as 19 pounds more for some heights. When I benchmarked myself against the old standards I was depressed, but now I am underweight or at least not over the maximum.

Business Process, Operational, and Support Service (50 points)

A company needs to identify quality improvement trends, based upon key measures of business processes, operations, and support services. These measures are the set of principal measurable services, including delivery and after-sales services, which, taken together, best represent the factors that predict customer satisfaction and quality in customer use.

- Accuracy
- Appearance
- Behavior
- Delivery
- Documentation
- Performance
- Reliability
- Timeliness

With these data available, one should be able to explain adverse trends and outline what steps the company has taken or plans to take to prevent a recurrence.

Supplier Quality Results (40 points)

The need for quality suppliers is critical. A company needs to understand its supplier's quality improvement trends related to the supplies and services provided. The supplies it provides are the starting blocks from which a company's own quality is achieved.

It's a funny thing about life:
If you refuse to accept anything but the very best
you will very often get it.

W. Somerset Maugham

Today the trends are not in percent accepted, but in PPM defective. Industry is reducing its supplier base to only certain high-quality suppliers. That is the first step in achieving high-quality products or services.

The quality of a product is only as good as
its weakest supplier.

Suppliers and customers need to have a high quality rating to survive. You cannot be like a parent who says, "Do as I say, not as I do." Suppliers now go into their customer's facilities and see if they "walk their talk"; if the customer's drive to improve quality is equal to or more intense than the demands they are putting on the supplier. Motorola and Xerox are walking their talk.

- Motorola advertises 6 sigma quality (PPM of 0.0018)
- Xerox says it has a PPM of 300 (1.2 sigma)

A company without a solid supplier base
is like a coach without a team.

A world-class company will have a proactive relationship with and will support its supplier base, much like parents do during the development of their children. The company will be a key factor in assisting its supplier in quality and productivity improvement areas. Additionally the company will have developed a system of awards and recognition for key suppliers.

Customer Satisfaction (300 points)

The customer satisfaction category examines a company's knowledge of the customer, overall customer service systems, responsiveness, and ability to meet requirements and expectations. Also examined are current levels and trends in customer satisfaction.

Determining Customer Requirements and Expectations (30 points)

Knowledge of customer requirements and expectations is more than a marketing tool; it is essential for improving your product or service quality. All too often we only look at the contract requirements or advertised performance. A company needs to listen to its customers.

The late James Burrill Angell, president of the University of Michigan for 38 years, was once asked for the secret of his success. He replied, "Grow antennae, not horns."

Antennae need to be close enough to receive a signal; therefore, we need to personally know our customers. We need to go where our product or service is being used or consumed. A physician cannot check the pulse of a patient without personal contact.

As with a medical examination, we need to monitor key elements on a regular basis. For a physician to monitor the color of my eyes and hair would be a nuisance and not profitable. In like manner monitoring nonessential elements will upset the customer and be of no value. Choose the elements carefully so that both you and the customer can appreciate your motivation.

When gathering this information, the company needs to recognize that the buyer of a product or service may not be the end user. Thus, when identifying customer groups, take into account both the buyer and the end user.

The customer's opinion is not solely based on the performance of the product or service. It also includes experience during purchase, delivery, and after-sales service. These factors influence the customer's preference and view of quality.

Customer Relationship Management (50 points)

This category identifies how a company must effectively manage its customer relationships so that continuous improvement is ensured.

Quality Creed
We shall strive for excellence in all endeavors.
We shall set our goals to achieve total customer satisfaction
and to deliver defect-free premium-value products on time,
with service second to none.

The above quality creed is only platitudes if the customer doesn't experientially understand the company's commitment.

Large companies have a difficult time communicating customer requirements to the appropriate levels. They have an equally difficult time obtaining information necessary to respond to customer inquiries or complaints.

This communication bottleneck is like dealing with a large medical group as opposed to a family doctor to whom you have gone for years. Somehow the access to and response from the large groups is slow and impersonal.

Regardless of a company's size, it needs to establish a system that provides each customer with a clear method of communication, including reliable follow-up to each inquiry. This normally doesn't involve the addition of more people.

Several companies have empowered customer-contact employees to resolve problems promptly and to take extraordinary measures when appropriate. These employees are selected not only on their technical and business knowledge, but also, and possibly more importantly, on their cooperative and professional attitude when dealing with difficult problems.

One test of good manners
is to be able to put up pleasantly with bad ones.

These customer-contact employees, although a single-point contact, are provided with an infrastructure of technical and logistic support that enables them to obtain a quick response. The information gained by these customer contacts, both positive and negative, is then analyzed and becomes a management tool for rewards and improvements.

Customer Service Standards (20 points)

- A business philosophy.

- In order to be successful, we must sell goods at a profit and still satisfy our customers.

- If we satisfy the customer but fail to get the profit, we will soon be out of business.

- If we get the profit but fail to satisfy the customer, we will soon be out of customers.

- The secret of doing both lies in one word: *service.* Service means doing something so valuable for the customers that they are glad to pay a price that allows us to make a profit.

A company needs this direct contact with the customer; however, there need to be standards so the contacts are done properly and in order. Helter-skelter contacts are annoying to the customer and internally a logistic nightmare.

These well-defined, objectively measurable standards need to be set and then modified (see PDCA, Chapter 6) so they continually meet the customer's requirements and expectations.

The monitoring and analysis of your service standards should be evaluated not only by customer feedback, but also by employee involvement. The employees who deal with the customers and those who see returned items have a wealth of information that needs to be tapped.

Commitment to Customers (15 points)

A company's commitment to customers and its explicit and implicit promises should be considered sacred.

*Without **continuity***
*you lose your **consistency**,*
*without **consistency***
*you lose your **credibility**,*
without credibility
*you end up losing your **customers**.*

Naylor Sargent

Product and service guarantees and product warranties need to be comprehensive, understandable, and credible. This is not a short-term or static commitment. A company needs to improve its product or service continuously so that its guarantees and warranties can also be enhanced.

Complaint Resolution for Quality Improvement *(25 points)*

Although customer complaints indicate you are not meeting your customers' needs or expectations, a progressive company will use complaints to its benefit. The company will investigate, resolve, and use the complaint information for quality improvement to prevent a recurrence. A system needs to be established that captures all complaints so their aggregate can be analyzed by a Pareto chart or some other means that focuses management's attention. Management can then marshal the resources needed to determine the underlying causes and make the necessary improvements to preclude a recurrence.

> *If the cause cannot be determined,*
> *the failure could not have happened.*

Customers know that a "no cause for rejection" response is seldom true. If the product was not faulty, the supplier is at fault for not providing the resources necessary to make that determination. If you badger the customer into saying it isn't your problem, you really have not won: A person convinced against his or her will is of the same opinion still.

Determining Customer Satisfaction *(20 points)*

A company wanting to know and measure customer satisfaction needs to develop a method or process for objectively making this determination. The information then needs to be used to constantly improve the customer's opinion. Some companies send out response cards with their products while others call or interview their customers directly. The personal contact, though costly, provides immediate and candid responses. This real-time information is valuable because you can make real-time corrections.

Progressive companies also seek customer satisfaction measurements on their competitors' products or services. This segment of benchmarking helps sharpen a company's quality improvement efforts.

The correlation of information on your and your competitors' products provides customer preferences in specific product features. Although this correlation is important, we need to focus on being the world leader, not on being competitive. We don't want to compete against poor health, we want to win and have exceptional health. At halftime Vince Lombardi didn't tell his team to make the necessary changes so that they could be competitive; he told them to *win!*

Customer Satisfaction Results *(70 points)*

The customer satisfaction results need to be analyzed continuously, including positive and negative data. The operative word is "continuously" since the needs and wants of customers change.

A company that made steam irons for cloths conducted a survey several years ago so that it could better understand its customers' needs and wants. It found that red irons sold much better in the South and heavier irons sold better all over the country. Neither one of these had any bearing on the actual use of the iron, but they are what the customer wanted.

This survey, however, was not a one-time occurrence. As customers became more knowledgeable, their wants and needs changed. Now lighter irons are preferred in most parts of the country.

Some of the adverse indicators that need to be analyzed are:

- Complaints
- Returns
- Refunds
- Downgrades
- Claims
- Repairs
- Replacements
- Warranty cost
- Warranty work
- Repeat services
- Mandatory recalls

Customer Satisfaction Comparison (70 points)

It is interesting to note that "customer satisfaction" is twice as important as the "quality assurance of products and services" according to this scoring. Doctors, in like manner, maintain their patients through "customer satisfaction."

A study showed that three out of four patients changed doctors because they were not comfortable with their bedside manner. The doctors wouldn't listen to the patients, and although they could treat their patients' physical needs, they did not treat their emotional needs. Consequently, the customer wasn't satisfied. This had nothing to do with their technical competence (quality of products), but the doctors didn't emotionally satisfy their customers.

A company's performance, as seen by its customer, needs to be constantly reviewed for the company's individual rating and how it compares with the competition. When a high level of achievement has been obtained and an award, plaque, or some other form of recognition is received, the company should celebrate. The very next day, however, a progressive company will look for more improvement opportunities.

Two indicators that tangibly indicate customer satisfaction are as follows:

1. *Benchmarking.* How does the company compare with its competition and world-class companies? Analyze where the company stood one, two, three, four, and five years ago; a continuously improving trend is the only acceptable trend.

2. *Product/service performance.* Review the customer's field experience and track the number of actual failures. Those who have adverse trends need to think long and hard about the number of customer problems.

C H A P T E R 5

INDICATORS/
SYMPTOMS
OF HEALTH

A complete medical examination, although personalized to some degree, has a base of indicators that provide clues to one's overall health. In like manner, company examination, though tailored to the specific industry, has a base of diagnostics that indicate its overall health.

Table 5: Indicators/Symptoms

Company	Personal
Inventory	Weight
Housekeeping	Hygiene
Maturity	Age
Throughput	Pulse
Contracts	Hearing and vision
Training	Heart
Customer responsiveness	Reflexes
Process capability	Internal organs
Tooling	Teeth and muscles
Trends	X-rays
Waste process and disposal	Bowel and urine samples
Supplier input	Diet/nutrition
Capacity	Lungs
Management	Brain

INVENTORY (Weight)

When a person walks through the door you immediately know whether their weight is excessive. Likewise, when you walk through a shop you have a good idea if its inventory is excessive.

A person's acceptable weight is determined by a number of factors: sex, height, bone structure, age, and occupation (athletic, nonathletic). Those with excess weight generally have a higher health risk and shorter life expectancy.

In like manner, an acceptable inventory level is a factor of many variables: customized products, high production, electronics, aftermarket support, and so on. A good way to determine your inventory is through benchmarking world-class companies that have a similar technology/product. A successful company will strive to make its inventory turns higher than the industry leaders. Those failing to reduce their inventory by increased inventory turns will lose market share and have a shorter life expectancy.

We are comfortable using the pull system for office supplies because we know suppliers that can fill our orders quickly. A world-class company will develop suppliers that can fill their product orders quickly. This confidence is not easily obtained. A company needs to work closely with its suppliers both with manufacturing process and product/service design (concurrent engineering).

HOUSEKEEPING (Hygiene)

Individuals who don't take care of their personal hygiene often have a poor health record. This relationship is normally true within industry; poor housekeeping yields poor quality.

Before an audit, most companies will make an extra effort to clean their facilities. This may provide a false impression. I know an individual who has a fairly reliable method of inspecting a company's true attitude toward housekeeping. This person goes to a washroom used by the production employees; the maintenance and aesthetics of the washroom is closely related to the normal housekeeping. Additionally, it is an indication of the respect management has for the production worker.

MATURITY (Age)

The maturity of a product or company has a direct relationship to the inventory. There is a reverse analogy with the acceptable weight for people over 35 and those between 18 and 35. The more mature a product or company is, the lower, not higher, its inventory level should be.

THROUGHPUT (Pulse)

One of the first items on a physical examination is your pulse. If the blood is not effectively circulating through your body, deterioration will occur. In like manner, if products are not flowing smoothly through a company's manufacturing process, its life expectancy is reduced. Products need to efficiently flow through to the shipping dock in order to maintain revenue.

CONTRACTS (Hearing and Vision)

A visual inspection of a person's hearing and vision will identify any apparent physical problems. This is not, however, the total examination. How these senses actually function is the ultimate test. We need to check not only the proceduralized system but also the implementation.

A company may have an elaborate system for reviewing a contract or purchase order. That, however, is just the beginning. The contractual requirements need to be effectively translated and adhered to by the applicable departments.

TRAINING (Heart)

Just like the heart delivers life-sustaining blood to the entire body, so a company's training activity provides the lifeblood to its most valuable asset: the employees.

If you think training is expensive,
try ignorance.

As the blood needs constant nourishment to maintain its value to your muscles, so people need to be kept current with technology. This need for training permeates the whole company. The following is a limited list of the training categories that constantly need refreshing:

- Management — motivational skills
- Office — word processing
- Production — new equipment and skills
- Engineers — accounting laws

- Environmental — government laws
- New technology — new technology and laws

CUSTOMER RESPONSIVENESS (Reflexes)

The responsiveness to customer orders, inquiries, and complaints is a direct reflection on the efficiency of an organization and its focus on the customer. A doctor would be concerned if after tapping a patient's knee with a mallet he or she responded five minutes later. There would be something seriously wrong with the nervous system. There aren't many people who would care to ride in your car with such slow reflexes and there wouldn't be many customers who would like to rely on a company with slow customer reflexes.

PROCESS CAPABILITY (Internal Organs)

During my annual physical I am subjected to a battery of tests that evaluate how my vital organs are functioning. My health is directly affected by my internal processing, which cannot be reliably evaluated by an external inspection.

The special processes also need regular monitoring to ensure that they are still under control. Inspection of the final product is not economical and sometimes cannot verify the results of a special process:

- *Heat treat.* Quality is only assured by control of the process. Hardness checks, for quench-hardening steels, are only an indication of quality; without process control, quality cannot be assured. A part that has an out-of-specification atmosphere during the hardening cycle could pass the hardness inspections and have an unacceptable tensile strength.

- *Forging.* The grain flow of a forged part is assured by strict adherence to many process controls. Industry must rely on these controls, as destructive inspections cannot economically be done in every case.

TOOLING (Teeth and Muscles)

Just as humans need teeth and muscles to process nourishment, so a company needs the proper tooling to efficiently process the parts received from suppliers.

TRENDS (X-rays)

During an examination I normally receive an X-ray. This is a method of identifying and pinpointing any other internal concerns.

Walking through a company I often suspect a problem when I see poor housekeeping, excess inventory, large rework area, and so on. When I evaluate the company's trends (throughput, Cpk's, PPM defective, and so on), I am then able to pinpoint more closely the area that needs attention.

WASTE PROCESS AND DISPOSAL (Bowel and Urine Samples)

Prior to my annual physical I am put on a diet and then required to provide samples of my waste disposal system. We can draw two analogies to this: the environmental concerns over industrial waste disposal and the processing and disposition of nonconforming items.

SUPPLIER INPUT (Diet/Nutrition)

People are what they eat. Those who live on junk food cannot expect good health. Those companies that knowingly or unknowingly (ignorance is no excuse) accept defective products from their suppliers cannot expect to provide high quality to their customers.

The supplier's quality needs to be consistent. A supplier that provides inconsistent quality cannot be relied upon.

CAPACITY (Lungs)

A company that over-commits its resources turns into a patient with respiratory problems. When the person has to exert extra energy he or she becomes short of breath and quickly fades away; the person cannot keep up with the task before him or her.

MANAGEMENT (Brain)

All too often we look at the above results when most often it is management that directs the activity just like the brain directs our actions with the results affecting our body, not our brain.

C H A P T E R   6

INDUSTRIAL PRESCRIPTIONS AND DIAGNOSTIC TOOLS

Doctors who only identify a health problem or risk have not fulfilled their Hippocratic oath. They also need to prescribe a way to arrest, reduce, and ultimately eliminate the problem, if at all possible.

Yesterday's industry responded to quality problems by increasing inspection. This only camouflaged a problem from the customer, much like aspirin and drugs don't cure a person but hide the symptoms. While inspection and aspirin have their place, the quality professional must use the tools that diagnose the root cause and identify a cure. There is a vast number of quality tools available and like the doctor or pharmacist, the quality professional needs to identify the proper one and explain when and how to employ it.

When a prescription or health program is recommended I don't automatically understand how to implement the program or what to expect during and after completion. The medications and programs are foreign to me, the uninformed patient. Fortunately the doctor or pharmacist takes great pains to explain the various aspects of his or her program or prescription.

Industry hasn't been as professional in its follow-through. We believe everybody knows what we are referring to when we recommend one of the better known systems/programs shown in Figure 4. Unfortunately most people don't really know the basics and are too embarrassed to ask.

The following section is a brief overview of some of the more popular tools we "quality doctors" are prescribing. We should be as familiar with these and other tools as we expect our doctors to be with their prescriptions. If you have a thorough knowledge of these tools, don't pat yourself on the back. We are in a dynamic industry that is constantly changing. Don't assume you know all the necessary tools or you will be as myopic as Charles Duell, director of the U.S. Patent Office in 1899, who said, "Everything that can be invented has been invented."

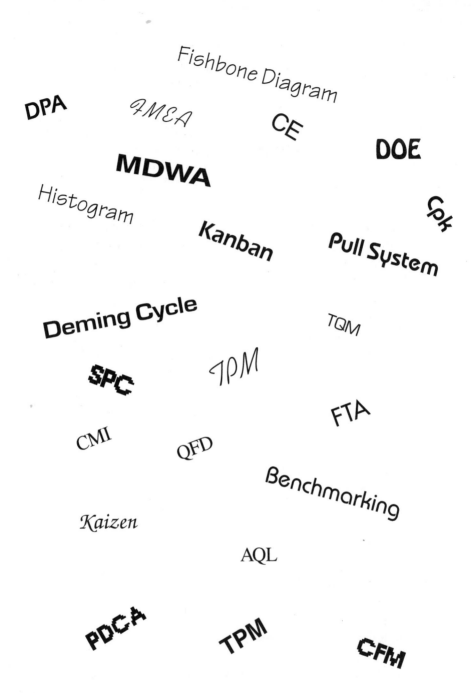

Figure 4: Industrial Prescriptions and Diagnostic Tools

Affinity Diagram

The affinity diagram is used to organize a large number of ideas, opinions, issues, or other concerns into groupings based on the natural relationships that exist among them. The process is designed to stimulate creativity and participation. It works best in groups of limited size (maximum of eight members recommended) in which members are accustomed to working together. This tool is often used to organize ideas generated by brainstorming.

Procedure

1. State the issue in broad terms (details may prejudice the responses).
2. Record individual responses on small cards.
3. Mix the cards and spread them randomly on a large table.
4. Group related cards together:
   - Sort cards that seem to be related into groups.
   - Limit number of groupings to 10 without forcefitting single cards into groups.
   - Locate or create a header card that captures the meaning of the group.
   - Place this header card on top.
5. Transfer the information from cards onto paper, outlined by groupings.

Acceptable Quality Level

Acceptable quality level (AQL) is the maximum percent defective considered acceptable for acceptance sampling purposes. Sometimes this is referred to as "a quick look."

Arrow Diagram

This is often used in PERT (program evaluation and review technique) and CPM (critical path method). It uses a network representation to show the steps necessary to implement a plan.

Arrow diagrams are combinations of the famous "time line" Gantt charts of traditional business and flowcharts. Arrow diagrams are used to show all of the relationships between process actions in terms of sequence, interrelationships, and time. An arrow diagram is a Gantt chart with a process orientation.

Benchmarking

Benchmarking is the process of continually comparing a company's performance on critical customer requirements against the best in the industry (direct competitors) or class (companies recognized for superiority in performing certain functions) in order to establish priorities and targets that will lead to a competitive advantage in the marketplace.

Procedure

1. Determine what items to benchmark. The items should be key characteristics of your process output directly related to your customers' needs.

2. Determine what to benchmark: companies, organizations, or groups that are direct competitors and/or noncompetitors with the "best-in-class" reputation and key similarities such as:

   – Type of process, such as billing and shipping.

   – Characteristics/nature of work, such as type of customers, size, and outputs.

3. Determine benchmarks:

   – Collect data by means of direct contact, surveys, interviews, personal and professional contacts, technical journals, advertisements, and so on.

   – Analyze the data.

66

4. For each benchmark item just identified, determine the "best-in-class" target for direct competitors and noncompetitors.

Requirements are based on both customer needs and benchmarking targets.

  — If the results of benchmarking determine that direct competitors' performance exceeds your customers' needs, then your requirements must be at least as good as the best direct competitor targets.

  — If the results of benchmarking determine that no direct competitors achieve your customers' needs, and if noncompetitors also do not achieve customer needs, then you should reevaluate your customer needs.

Seven Benefits of Benchmarking

1. Creating a culture that values continuous improvement to achieve excellence.

2. Enhancing creativity by devaluing the "not-invented-here" syndrome.

3. Increasing sensitivity to changes in the external environment.

4. Shifting the corporate mind-set from relative complacency to a strong sense of urgency for ongoing improvement.

5. Focusing resources through performance targets jointly set with employees.

6. Prioritizing the areas to work on first.

7. Sharing the best practices between benchmarking partners.

Cause-and-Effect Diagram

A cause-and-effect diagram is also known as the fishbone or Ishikawa diagram, named after Dr. Kaoru Ishikawa who developed it in Japan in 1943. The cause-and-effect diagram can be a significant aid in identifying factors that might need control in a process (see Figure 5).

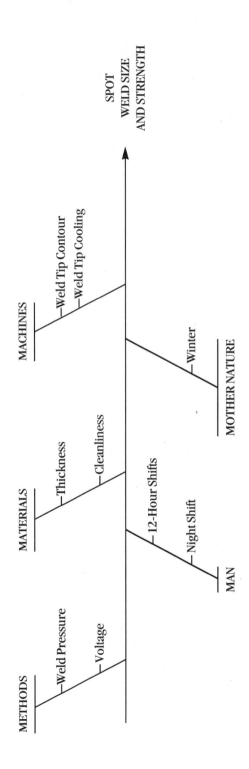

Figure 5: Cause-and-Effect Diagram

1. Draw a long straight horizontal line to represent the process.

2. Establish a branch arrow to the horizontal line for each major contributor (*method, material, machinery, man* or human factors, *mother nature* or environment) to the process.

3. Establish smaller twigs to each significant factor's branch arrows, representing factors contributing to the significant factor.

The diagram creates a systematic analysis of all factors that contribute to a process and, therefore, can be very valuable in identifying factors that could have an important effect on the final product.

Concurrent Engineering

Concurrent engineering (CE) is a systematic approach to the integrated, concurrent design of products and their related processes, including manufacture and support. This approach is intended to cause the developers to consider from the outset all elements of the product life cycle from conception through disposal, including quality, cost, schedule, and user requirements. A better name for CE is integrated process development as it involves the whole organization and supplier base during the design phase; it isn't an engineering program.

The National Institute of Standards & Technology, Thomas Group Inc., Institute for Defense Analyses has attributed the following improvements to CE:

- Development time: 30 – 70 percent less
- Engineering changes: 65 – 90 percent fewer
- Time to market: 20 – 90 percent less
- Overall quality: 200 – 600 percent higher
- White-collar productivity: 20 – 110 percent higher
- Dollar sales: 5 – 50 percent higher
- Return on assets: 20 – 120 percent higher

To make optimum use of CE the team should focus on the following basic design principles to achieve the lowest life cycle costs:

1. Design for reduced part count.

2. Design for fewer processes.

3. Design for low-complexity processes.

4. Design for minimum part and assembly handling.

5. Design for easy access and visibility by operators.

6. Eliminate and/or commonize fasteners.

7. Design out opportunities for incorrect assembly.

8. Design for interlocking parts.

9. Design for easy part handling.

10. Design the process for minimum transport.

Continuous Flow Manufacturing

Continuous flow manufacturing (CFM) is an ongoing process requiring an optimally balanced line to achieve the lowest cost, defect-free product. The CFM approach to process improvement is that:

- The work content in each process or operation should be comparable to allow a continuous flow of the product.

- The rate of production should equal the rate of consumption.

- Any process or operation that does not add value is waste and should be eliminated, for example transportation, counting, issuing, retrieving, storage/buffer, inspection, rework, and so on. When waste is identified, an action plan should be put in place to eliminate these nonvalue-added processes or operations.

- Focus is put on the use of the human resource. The use of machines is not a major factor. Machines and equipment are depreciated over time and eventually they are free except for the space they occupy and maintenance costs they incur. Human resources, on the other hand, continue to get more expensive, salaries and benefits continue to increase, and investments are continually made through education and training.

Continuous Measurable Improvement

Continuous measurable improvement (CMI) is another form of TQM. The difference is that there is accountability through a measurement system. The company can objectively determine if its TQM is truly in *word* and *deed.*

Cpk

Cpk is a capability ratio that compares engineering specification to the spread in the output of the process accounting for centering (Figure 6).

$$\text{Cpk} = \text{Smaller of} \left[\frac{\text{USL} - \text{Avg}}{3 \, \text{Sigma}} \, , \, \frac{\text{Avg} - \text{LSL}}{3 \, \text{Sigma}} \right]$$

Avg = Average of measurements

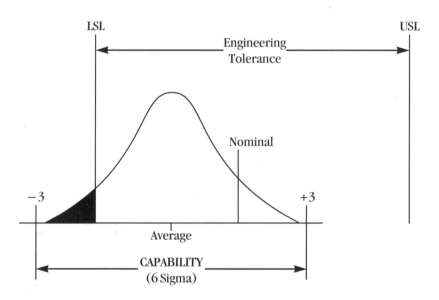

Figure 6: Cpk: A Capability Ratio

Deming Cycle

This is how PDCA is identified in Japan; W. Edwards Deming introduced them to this process. See the plan-do-check-act section for an explanation of the Deming Cycle.

Design of Experiments

Design of experiments (DOE) is a technique of reducing the variability in the output of a process. Defining those parameters that have an effect on the final product and conducting a set of experiments that will optimize the desired result versus variation of parameters. This technique is frequently used when the process has a low Cpk.

Destructive Physical Analysis

Destructive physical analysis (DPA) is most often used on a component level part, where the part is physically dissected in an attempt to find construction flaws and anomalous "maverick" phenomena not detectable in tests.

Fishbone Diagram

See *Cause-and-Effect Diagram,* page 68.

Failure Mode and Effect Analysis

A failure mode and effect analysis (FMEA) is a methodical system that examines all the ways in which a failure may occur. For each potential failure, an estimate is made of its effect on the total system and of its seriousness. In addition, a review is made of the action being taken (or planned) to minimize the probability of failure or to minimize the effect of failure.

This method requires that you identify every part of a product or sequence in a system and answer the following questions:

1. What defect in this item could possibly cause a failure?

2. What would cause this item to fail?

3. What type of failure is it? For a part, it could be a hydraulic failure (H), mechanical failure (M), wear failure (W), customer abuse (C), and so on.

4. What is the probability that this item will fail? (1 = very low to 5 = very high)

5. How serious would this failure be to the operation of the product? (1 = very low to 5 = very high)

6. What would be the effect of the failure on the product?

7. What are the alternatives or ways in which you could prevent or reduce the probability of failure?

This analysis identifies the areas into which you should invest your resources to obtain the greatest improvement.

Fault Tree Analysis

In fault tree analysis (FTA) the starting point is the list of deficiencies for which the designer must provide some solution. This list is prepared from records of actual discrepancies. Each discrepancy on the list then becomes a failure mode requiring analysis. The analysis then considers the possible direct causes that could lead to the event. Next, it looks for the origins of these causes. Finally, it looks for ways to avoid these origins and causes. The branching out of origins and causes is what gives the technique the name "fault tree" analysis. This approach is the reverse of FMEA which starts with origins and causes and looks for any resulting bad effects.

Histogram

A histogram is a graphic form of frequency distribution using rectangles whose widths represent class intervals and whose heights represent the corresponding frequencies. The diagram provides an easily comprehensible static picture of how a system is presently operating. It provides a quick method for viewing how an improvement effort in an area is going. It can also be used to detect abnormalities in a process or activity.

There are a variety of patterns (Figure 7) that are like fingerprints. They point out the probable cause of the distribution.

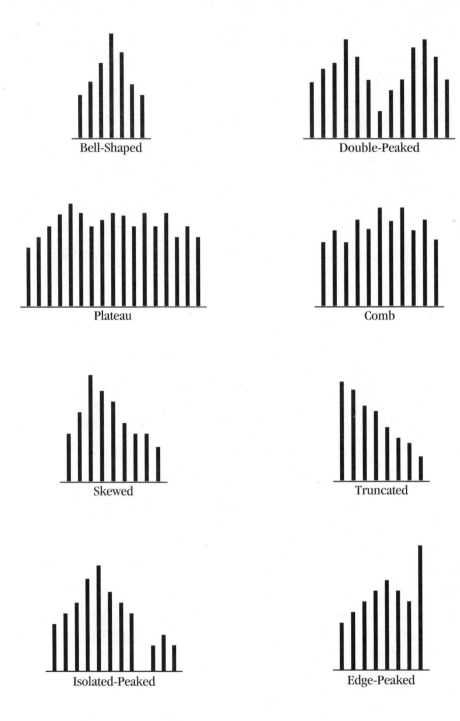

Figure 7: Common Histogram Patterns

- *Bell-shaped* This is the normal and desirable distribution of data.

- *Double-peaked* This indicates that there are two distinct processes causing this distribution.

- *Plateau* This is similar to the double-peaked distribution; however, there are several distinct processes causing this distribution.

- *Comb* There was probably a measurement error or the data were modified either by grouping or rounding off the data.

- *Skewed* This indicates that the average reading is near the process limitation (short side), which only permits variation on the long side.

- *Truncated* This is similar to the skewed pattern; however, one side is on the absolute limit of the process.

- *Isolated-peaked* This is similar to the double-peaked distribution; however, the short, bell shape indicates something that doesn't happen often.

- *Edge-peaked* This is similar to the comb in that there is probably an error in the data. One may have grouped all the readings past a certain point into one value.

Kaizen

Kaizen is a Japanese word meaning improvement. When applied to the workplace, Kaizen means continuing improvement that involves everyone, managers and workers alike. Moreover, it means continuing improvement in personal, home, social, and work life. Kaizen means gradual, unending improvement, doing "little things" better, and setting and achieving ever higher standards.

Kanban

Kanban is a physical container, marked floor area, or other device that holds a quantity of material equal to the predetermined lot size.

Keep It Simple, Sam

Keep it simple, Sam (KISS) is a philosophy we need to keep in mind when we are using some of the tools identified in this book. We can get so technologically oriented that we spend more time working the tools than we do solving the problems.

Loss Function

The concept of loss function states that any variation from a target value always results in some loss to the user. For example, at the next higher level of assembly, rework may be necessary to allow a component to fit properly. The final consumer may also experience loss through reduced performance or premature failure.

A continuous loss function illustrates economic losses owing to variation both within and outside the specification limits. Although the exact form of the loss function is generally unknown, approximating it with a simple curve is useful in conceptualizing the economic impact of variation on a given process (Figure 8).

Management by Wandering Around

This is a type of leadership management called management by wandering around (MBWA). To wander, with customers and suppliers and your own people, is to be in touch with what's really important. The number one managerial productivity problem in America is, quite simply, managers who are out of touch with their people and with their customers.

Worker attitude surveys invariably reveal that workers want to see their top bosses from time to time. Most top managers, however, remain closeted in their ivory towers, too busy with "more important" issues to meet with their people.

The object is not just for top managers to see and be seen. It is to mingle with their people on a regular basis, to get to know them, to take a personal interest in them, to extend that interest beyond the workplace to their family situations, even to helping with personal problems if these are volunteered by the employees. At first, workers in such encounters will tend to be shy and cautious. Having been looked down upon for so long, they are not likely to open up immediately. They

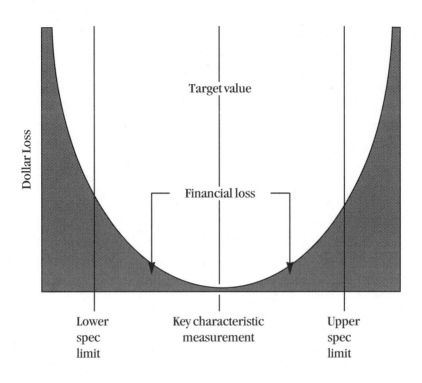

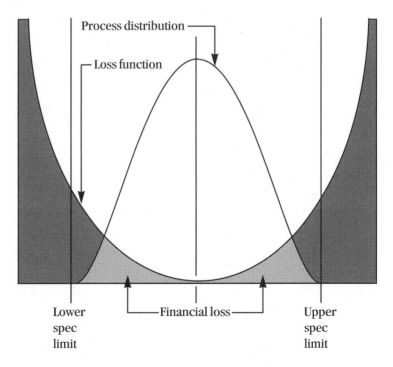

Figure 8: Loss Function

may even be suspicious of the manager's true motives. But once the door is opened, MBWA can replace fear with communication, trust, and enthusiasm. The good manager will listen. Having listened, he or she can turn gripes into constructive ideas. Having obtained constructive ideas, he or she can act on them. Having acted on them, the manager can give feedback, and in this way start an upward spiral of mutual confidence and respect.

Pareto's Law

The Pareto law is also referred to as the "vital few and trivial many" principle. This principle states that 20 percent of the customers/parts account for 80 percent of the sales/factory costs. Look at your supplier base and you will discover that 20 percent of your suppliers account for 80 percent of your purchased products. In like manner, when reviewing a quality system you will find that 80 percent is working fine, but the 20 percent that isn't affects the whole program.

When your heart, which is less then 20 percent of your body, isn't functioning properly your entire physical and mental state is adversely affected. The Pareto law allows the quality professional to get to the heart of the matter before other areas are adversely affected.

Pareto analysis is one of the most powerful of all management tools and is widely used as a means of attacking the bulk of the problem areas with the least amount of analytical study. (See Figure 9.)

Plan-Do-Check-Act

Plan-Do-Check-Act, or PDCA, is commonly known as the Shewhart Cycle. This was created by Walter A. Shewhart, one of the pioneers in statistical quality control. In Japan, it's known as the Deming Cycle because W. Edwards Deming described it to them. (See Figure 10.)

First, start with planning (P). Define the problem you are attacking, decide what data you need, how to get these data, and what you will do with them. Second, do (D) something. This could be getting the data you decided you needed, running a test, making a change, or whatever your plan calls for. Third, check (C) the results of your action. In some instances, this will be done by a control chart. In any event, evaluate the results and causes of variation. Histograms, Pareto charts, and scattergrams may be helpful at this stage. Fourth, analyze

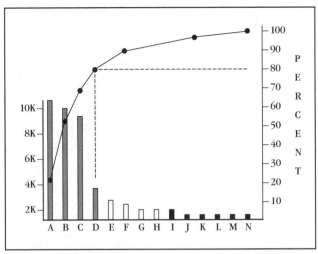

Eighty percent of the costs are associated with approximately 20 percent of the defect types, identifying which problems to solve first.

Figure 9: Pareto Diagram

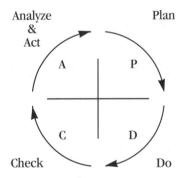

Figure 10: The Plan-Do-Check-Act Cycle

and act (A) on the data you obtained in the third step. Based on that you take appropriate action, which could be a process change or a decision that a new plan is needed.

Repeat the PDCA cycle. After you act, you go back to planning and start another cycle. Even if the first trip around was successful, there are always more opportunities waiting to be discovered. The cycle is really a spiral going upward to better and better quality.

Unfortunately, many believe that a process is fixed and PDCA should stand for "please don't change again."

Poka-Yoke

Poka-Yoke means mistake-proof; it is an inspection system that goes one step beyond "Murphy-proofing." For example, when an operator inadvertently makes an error, a sensor will notify the operator by turning on a light, ringing a buzzer, or even stopping production. There are two stages to poka-yoke. The first stage involves detecting an error that has taken place through sensing devices used by inspection. The second and more powerful stage involves preventing the operator from creating the error through the use of sensors that stop further processing.

Policy Deployment

Policy deployment (PD) is an excellent way to orchestrate continuous improvement throughout an organization by setting targets for the most critical continuous improvement tasks. In essence, it is applying the PDCA cycle to strategic quality improvement. PD is the process of determining key policies (annual and long-range targets and plans) throughout the company, from the highest to the lowest levels. These interdepartmental and intradepartmental "policies" need to be developed through negotiation between and across organizations so that the whole company is aware and supportive. This negotiation aspect makes PD more than simply management by objective (MBO).

While the specific steps actually used in PD vary considerably from company to company, the following six steps capture the essence of the general approach to PD:

1. Develop a five-year vision for the company.

2. Determine an annual policy in support of the vision.

3. Deploy the policy throughout the organization through participative planning.

4. Implement the policy.

5. Audit the process and plans monthly.

6. Audits are conducted by top management.

Process Capability

A process capability study is a systematic study of a process to determine its ability to meet specifications or tolerance limits. This study is conducted when trained, experienced operators are using approved instructions and specified raw materials. Over the course of this study there will be different operators, different lots of raw materials or components, tool wear, or other factors that may be affected by time.

The major purpose of this study is to discover whether a process is in a steady state and, if it is, whether the product will meet the customer's quality requirements.

A process is considered capable when the following are true:

1. The process is in stable statistical control.

2. It is where individual measurements are normally distributed.

3. It is where the process is adequately centered between specification limits (Figure 11).

4. It is where the area between ±4 standard deviations (Sigma) is equal to or less than specification limits (Figure 11).

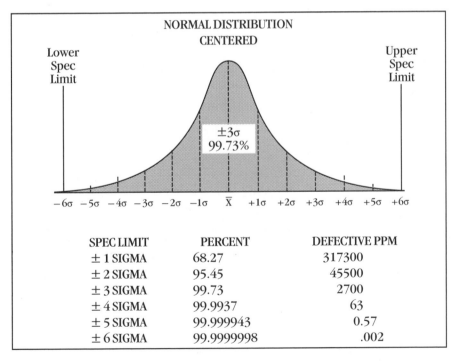

SPEC LIMIT	PERCENT	DEFECTIVE PPM
± 1 SIGMA	68.27	317300
± 2 SIGMA	95.45	45500
± 3 SIGMA	99.73	2700
± 4 SIGMA	99.9937	63
± 5 SIGMA	99.999943	0.57
± 6 SIGMA	99.9999998	.002

Figure 11: Centered/Controlled Process

Pull System

The pull system is a discipline that allows the production line to build only that which is needed to fill a firm customer order. Product is built or processed only as demanded by succeeding processes. The pull system should start at the end of the process and ripple back to the beginning of the process. In this way the wastes of batch production are eliminated.

Quality Function Deployment

Quality function deployment (QFD) is a system for translating consumer requirements into appropriate company requirements at each: research, design, development, and production processes. It deploys *customer requirements* into product characteristics, product characteristics into part characteristics, part characteristics into process characteristics, and process characteristics into *production.*

Scatter Diagram

A scatter diagram is a simple graphical technique for studying relationships between two sets of associated data. Data displayed by a scatter diagram form a cloud of dots. Relationships are inferred based on the shape of the cloud as depicted in the attached page.

The scatter diagram is useful in any situation when a discovery or a confirmation of relationships is important in carrying out quality improvement projects or activities (Figure 12).

Procedure

1. Collect paired data (x,y) between which the relationship is of interest. It is desirable to have about 30 pairs of data.

2. Find the minimum and maximum values of both x and y and graduate the horizontal (x) and vertical (y) axes. Use graph paper. Both axes should be of about equal length. The number of graduations should be between three and 10 per axes.

3. Plot the data on the graph paper. When the same data are obtained from different pairs, draw concentric circles or plot the second point in the immediate vicinity of the first.

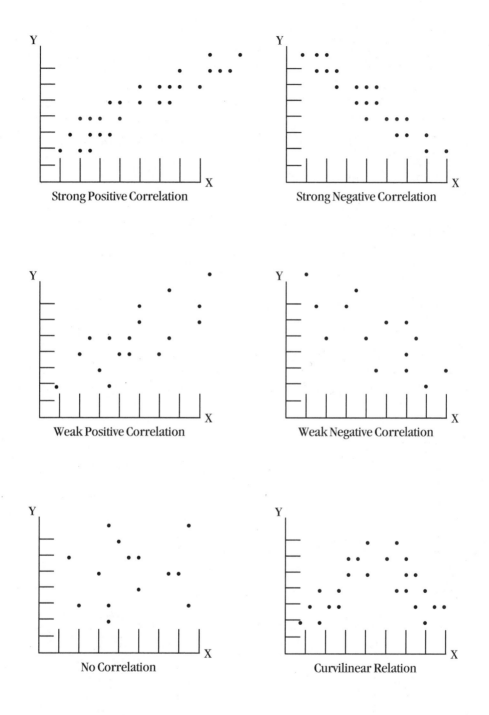

Figure 12: Scatter Diagram Configurations

4. Label the axes with characteristics they represent.

5. Examine the pattern (cloud) of dots to discover the type and the degree of relationship. Refer to the figures included on the attached page for interpretation of the patterns. Attention should be paid to outliers, that is, single or small clusters of dots that do not fit the general pattern. The presence of outliers indicates a presence of special causes that need to be investigated and removed.

Shewhart Cycle

See *PDCA*, page 000.

Standard Deviation

The standard deviation is used as the measure of spread for almost all industrial frequency distributions. It is the positive square root of the sum of the squared deviations of readings from their average divided by one less than the number of readings, or symbolically:

$$s = \sqrt{\frac{(X-\bar{X})^2 + (X-\bar{X})^2 + (X-\bar{X})^2 + \ldots + (X-\bar{X})^2}{n-1}}$$

Where s = sample standard deviation
$X \ldots X$ = value of each reading
$\bar{X}$ = average value of the series
n = number of readings

In the series 1, 2, 3, 4, 5, where the average is 3, the sample standard deviation can be calculated as follows:

$$s = \sqrt{\frac{(1-3)^2 + (2-3)^2 + (3-3)^2 + (4-3)^2 + (5-3)^2}{5-1}}$$

$$s = \sqrt{\frac{4 + 1 + 0 + 1 + 4}{4}} = \sqrt{\frac{10}{4}} = 1.58$$

Statistically the standard deviation (*s*) identifies the probability that readings will fall equally on either side of the average (Figure 13):

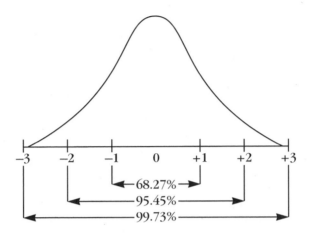

Figure 13: *Standardized Normal Distribution*

Statistical Process Control

Statistical process control (SPC) is the discipline of using control charts to monitor process output through time. Control charts are used to help identify sources of variation in a key characteristic or process where the two types of variations are common causes (inherent in a process), and special causes (having common assignable reasons).

Taguchi Loss Function Analysis

This is a quadratic equation used to quantify loss in monetary terms. The premise on which this equation was developed was that customers and manufacturers are not satisfied with manufacturing within the upper and lower specification limits. There are costs involved when manufacturing within limits but not achieving uniformity and consistency. The external losses include sales, warranty, and so on. The internal costs are inspection, test, analyzing, rework, and so on.

Total Preventive Maintenance

Total preventive maintenance (TPM) is a system that was developed by Toyota in the 1970s. This system mandates routine maintenance on machines and equipment, on a scheduled basis, in an attempt to avoid major repairs or breakdowns and assure repeatably accurate capabilities.

Those companies that believe the saying, "If it ain't broke, don't fix it," will yield nothing but equipment downtime, equipment inefficiencies, and high product defect rates.

Total Quality Management

Total quality management (TQM) is a concept of quality oriented toward total customer satisfaction. Together with reasonable costs of quality, TQM indicates the primary business and product planning and implementation goals and performance measurements of the marketing, engineering, production, industrial relations, and service functions of a company. TQM establishes customer satisfaction in quality and cost as its primary business goal. This is not some narrower technical goal restricted to a limited technical or production-oriented quality result.

X and R Charts

The average (X) and range (R) chart is a very sensitive control chart for tracking performance and identifying causes for unnatural fluctuations. These fluctuations from the average are visible even to the casual observer. Once a fluctuation is repeated, other statistical tools may be used to pinpoint the root cause and identify the corrective/preventative action.

CHAPTER 7

THE PROFESSIONAL'S EVALUATION

INSPECTION FREQUENCY

Individual Hypochondriacs

When children are first born and for the first few years, parents check their health regularly. They use a children's thermometer whenever the infant feels a little warm. When the infant cries they listen very carefully to assure themselves that it isn't a "serious" cry. Parents take these precautions because infants don't know what life is all about nor do they have the ability or knowledge to care for their own health. As they mature and begin to take care of their own hygiene, the parents relax their intensive health "inspection."

Unfortunately there are some people who never mature in this area. They think they are sick all the time and are forever taking their own temperature and visiting the doctor. We call these people "hypochondriacs." Taking care of their alleged illness makes them less productive, bothers those around them, and wastes the time of those in the medical profession, to say nothing of the waste of their personal finances.

Industrial Hypochondriacs

Today, too many companies are industrial hypochondriacs, inspecting products as a stopgap to assure defective products aren't delivered to the customer. While we need to assure the quality of products and services, constant inspection is a costly and antiquated way.

During development, new products often need to be inspected in great detail. As the product matures we unfortunately do not reassess the method of assuring quality; we continue to inspect everything.

(*Note:* There are programs, especially military programs, that contractually mandate a high level of inspection. This inspection may not be value added; however, it is contractual and the inspections must continue, unless the contract is revised.)

Physical hypochondriacs believe that they really have a chronic health problem and people just don't understand their constant need to consult with a doctor. Those who inspect a product to death are of the same opinion. They believe it is the only way to assure product quality. As we mature we need to put away childish activities.

As quality professionals, we need to encourage the entire operation to develop reliable process controls. There are many books on DOE, benchmarking, QFD, SPC, CE, and so on, that will help any company in its quest for process control.

AUDIT FREQUENCY

Unfortunately some companies establish a rigid audit schedule that is followed regardless of a department or supplier's performance. The company I work for has a set schedule for supplier evaluations. During this time we review the supplier's quality performance/rating, product volume, types of purchase orders, and type of processes. Based on an analysis of these data we decide if a complete or partial on-site audit is value added or if the objective evidence of quality is sufficient. We choose not to waste our time or the supplier's time by performing an audit just for the sake of performing an audit.

My annual physical examination is also based on whether it is value added. The doctor reviews my age, life-style, type of work, and medical history to determine how often and how in-depth my examination should be. Based on this analysis I didn't have a treadmill test this year and certain parts of the physical will not be repeated next year.

This same type of analysis is important when determining whether or not to perform an on-site audit. An unnecessary audit needlessly disturbs the supplier's production activity as well as your own relationship with the supplier.

EARLY NOTIFICATION

Early notification is a matter of common courtesy and respect for the auditee. Additionally it will help in establishing a positive relationship.

I have heard two reasons why we shouldn't let an auditee know about an impending audit too far in advance. The first is *quick fixes*. The auditor fears that the auditee will make corrections to its system prior to the audit and an accurate evaluation will not be obtained.

The purpose of an audit is to evaluate the degree of compliance. An early notification allows a supplier time to identify and correct deficiencies prior to the audit. As long as improvements are made, their motives are academic.

Doctors are pleased when people start a methodical exercise program well in advance of a physical. The patient's health is improved and the doctor really doesn't care whether the motive was to improve their health or to obtain a good medical report; in the end the objective of improved health was obtained.

The second is *special housekeeping,* in which the auditee will initiate a massive housekeeping activity that will camouflage its true condition.

This effort might camouflage less serious deficiencies but will rarely be sufficient to cover up any deep-rooted condition. This effort is similar to a patient wearing a tight belt so that he or she will appear thinner. It doesn't take long for the doctor to realize that the patient needs to lose some weight.

I appreciate a company that does some housekeeping prior to my arrival. I am less distracted by surface conditions and am able to concentrate on areas that have a greater effect on contract compliance. Prior to my annual physical I am asked to stay on a specific diet. As with housekeeping this removes some distractions so the doctor is able to concentrate on more important areas.

GENERAL INFORMATION AND PREPARATION

The auditee needs to know in advance when an audit will be performed so that he or she can prepare properly. Suppliers don't like to be surprised, especially when you show up at their front door ready to perform an audit. A surprise like this will ruin any possibility of establishing a good rapport.

How would you feel if your boss came to your office and insisted that you undergo a medical examination right away? You would be angry at your boss, your work schedule would be disrupted, and your attitude would be anything but pleasant.

The auditor, whether for an internal or a supplier audit, should contact the auditee to avoid any surprises. The following information should be communicated so that the auditee can make the necessary preparations.

Reason for the Audit. The scope of the audit needs to be clearly understood by both the auditee and the auditor. Preparation for a total systems audit is much different than when the customer is investigating a specific problem. (Preparation for an annual physical is much different than preparing for a biopsy of a suspected cancerous tumor.) This is not to say that one is less serious to the auditee than the other. In the eyes of the auditee there isn't an insignificant audit. As a famous surgeon put it, "Minor operations are those performed on other people."

Audit Schedule. The audit schedule should be coordinated as much as is practical with the auditee so that it causes the least amount of disruption to the operation. Scheduling appointments or audits often requires a great deal of coordination with both parties. The busier they are, the more difficult it is to schedule an audit. We are all familiar with the adage, "the customer is always right." The doctor's/auditor's schedule most often takes precedence. Although the auditor has the horsepower, he or she will be a guest at the auditee's facility and should try to accommodate the time most convenient for them.

Information Needed. Prior to performing an audit it is desirable to ask the auditee to complete the audit form in advance and send the completed form along with a copy of the company's quality manual back to the auditor. This exercise has many benefits.

1. The auditee better understands what is expected and can make the necessary corrections in advance.

2. The auditee is able to identify more efficiently the company procedures that satisfy specific requirements and can annotate these procedures on the audit form. This saves time for both parties. It is similar to the nurse who asks the patient in advance to answer questions that would take the medical staff a great deal of research to answer.

3. The basic information provides the auditor with an appreciation as to the size and complexity of the company. This information and self-analysis will enable the auditor/doctor to estimate how long the audit/physical will take.

4. The auditor is able to review the quality manual in advance of the audit. This saves time and provides some insight into the auditee's sophistication.

5. The auditor/doctor is able to concentrate on specific areas during the evaluation that appear to be especially vulnerable.

6. This information also allows the auditor/doctor to tailor the evaluation around the supplier's/patient's specific needs.

REVIEW HISTORY

The auditor should review the supplier's history prior to performing the audit. A great deal of insight can be gained by reviewing a supplier's previous performance. This includes the supplier's quality rating, delivery rating, and corrective action responses. Prior to going to the supplier, specific concerns can be identified that may be used as a vehicle to evaluate the supplier's quality system/program: verification that a corrective action is still in effect, incorporation of engineering changes on the purchase order has been accomplished, and so on.

An auditor receives more respect from a supplier when he or she has taken the time to become familiar with the supplier's product and history. The supplier perceives that the auditor is truly interested in the company and that the audit wasn't just another assignment.

Prior to an annual physical the doctor reviews last year's results and, coupled with any job change or other major event, uses that information to more thoroughly evaluate my physical condition. This preparation by the doctor goes a long way toward establishing a respectful rapport with me as well as developing a value-added physical examination plan. The preparation also gives the auditor/doctor an air of confidence.

CUSTOMIZING THE AUDIT WORKSHEETS

The basic groundwork has now been performed and the auditor has received both the completed worksheet and quality manual from the supplier. A review of these coupled with last year's audit and the supplier's current performance will identify areas that may require special attention. I have never audited a supplier the second time and followed the exact same worksheet. I used the same worksheet but I deliberately spent less time in some areas and more time in others. This is not an arbitrary change; the information I gathered during my preparation indicated continued good performance in some areas and a decline in others.

Last year's physical was not the same as this year's physical. My health was so good that the doctor didn't waste his time or mine by putting me on the treadmill. He did, however, customize the examination that allowed him to spend more time examining my eyes and talking about my weight, both areas that needed attention.

VARIETY OF AUDIT WORKSHEETS

We have been focusing on the comparison of a normal medical examination to a quality system audit. Both professions, however, have many more specialized worksheets.

My company has two volumes of process worksheets designed to evaluate compliance to specific military and industry specifications. Likewise, our medical department has approximately 20 types of examinations ranging from the executive physical, preemployment physical, noise exposure (required by Occupational, Safety and Health Administration), eye exam (required by contract), lung exam (company requirement for individuals performing certain processing operations), and so on.

IN-BRIEFING

The supplier should have already been informed about the audit: who will perform it, how long it will take, and what type of audit it will be. The in-briefing, a meeting with the auditee's management prior to conducting the audit, will quickly reiterate this information, establish lines of communication, and obtain permission to speak with those actively fulfilling the requirements of the purchase order, including hourly and salaried personnel. Failure to obtain this cooperation will significantly reduce the value of the audit.

The most important task for the auditor during the in-briefing is to establish a rapport with the auditee. The auditor should communicate by his or her mannerisms that he or she is a guest, willing and able to help the auditee. The auditor needs to exemplify a peaceable, considerate, and humble attitude.

Before this year's physical, my doctor talked briefly about last year's results, asked me questions about my current condition, explained what would take place during the physical, and asked permission to perform a proctoscope and treadmill test. If I didn't honestly answer his questions or give permission to perform specific aspects of the physical, my current health would not have been thoroughly evaluated.

PERFORM AUDIT

Desk audits and long lunches are unacceptable. The auditor must take control of the audit without being domineering, pushy, and arrogant. The auditor should have a plan in mind and follow it as quickly and efficiently as possible.

It would be a wasted exercise if I went to a doctor who sat behind his or her desk the entire time he or she claimed to be giving me a medical examination. It would also be a waste of time if I tried to direct the examination process.

During the audit it is best to document results as they are determined. This prevents the auditor from forgetting to obtain supportive information or documenting some of the detail.

DEFICIENCIES

Concerns identified during the course of an audit should be investigated. There is, however, a problem with auditors who over-investigate areas.

If you look at a problem with excessive magnification, eventually all you see is the space between molecules.

Andrew S. Grove, in his book *One-on-One with Andy Grove* (New York: Putnam, 1987), wrote:

Decisions sprung on others without warning tend to provoke opposition. Try taking more time in the early stages of your decision-making process. Talk to your colleagues about your pending decision before you make up your mind. Solicit and consider their views.

Discuss various alternatives with them and listen to their reactions. When you have arrived at a definite conclusion, visit with them again and tell them what you have decided and why. Then – and only then – make your announcement.

This elaborate process may seem like a waste of time to you at first, but I think you'll find that it will save time in the long run. You'll probably end up with a better decision and one that has support, or at least no opposition, from your coworkers. Such decisions will consequently be easier to implement.

EXIT BRIEFING

At the conclusion of an audit, the auditor should review all the findings to ensure proper understanding by the auditee. The more serious findings should be discussed in more detail explaining the possible ramifications if the deficiency is not corrected.

The areas audited that were found to be above average should also be highlighted at this time. To quote a renowned professional in her field, Mary Poppins, "A spoonful of sugar helps the medicine go down."

The doctor reviews the outcome of my physical in some detail. I feel good about the positive news and sometimes anxious about the negative. Fortunately, the doctor doesn't coldly tell me about a serious malady. I am given insight and council that allows me to partner with him in the corrective action. Those maladies that require additional resources are explained and recommendations given. As auditors, we should also provide council to our "patients" when appropriate.

AUDIT REPORT

The auditor should send an audit report to the supplier in accordance with a mutually understood time frame. Even if there were no deficiencies, this report needs to be sent. The company doctor provides me with a written report after each physical and I use it as a baseline during the year. I compare the results year to year to identify positive and negative trends. This same type of analysis is valuable to both the auditor and the supplier.

C H A P T E R 8

THE PATIENT'S
CORRECTIVE
ACTION

CORRECTIVE ACTIONS

Corrective action is defined as action taken to eliminate the causes of an existing undesirable deviation or nonconformity to prevent recurrence.

Requirement

We ask for corrective action when a serious or systemic deficiency is noted, not for every anomaly identified. Our actions should communicate to the supplier that we truly are there to help. When we pick apart every little deficiency we become a thorn in the side, which is quite different from the touch of a rose petal.

   I am sure that the doctor found some minor areas that could be improved but weren't significant enough to mention. The only suggestion was that I exercise regularly and lose 10 to 15 pounds. I appreciated the sensitivity in which he presented these suggestions and also that he didn't laboriously review every little insignificant problem he found.

Cause

Before effective corrective action can be implemented, a careful evaluation must be made of the conditions that caused the problem. Often, one cause may be responsible for several deficiencies.

   An initial cause may not be it. We should ask "Why?" not once but five times. Often, the first answer to a problem is not the root cause. Asking "Why?" several times will reveal several causes, one of which is usually the root cause.

For every complex question
there is a simple answer
*and it's **wrong**.*

H. L. Mencken

The following is an example of finding the root cause of a machine stoppage.[1]

Question 1: Why did the machine stop?

Answer 1: Because the fuse blew due to an overload.

Question 2: Why was there an overload?

Answer 2: Because the bearing lubrication was inadequate.

Question 3: Why was the lubrication inadequate?

Answer 3: Because the lubrication pump was not functioning properly.

Question 4: Why wasn't the lubricating pump working properly?

Answer 4: Because the pump axle was worn out.

Question 5: Why was it worn out?

Answer 5: Because sludge got in.

By asking "Why?" five times, it was possible to identify the real cause and hence the real solution: attaching a strainer to the lubricating pump. If the people had not gone through such repetitive questions, they might have settled with an intermediate countermeasure, such as replacing the fuse.

Solution

Once the conditions that caused the problem have been identified, possible solutions must be determined and implemented. The following questions will help determine the appropriate solution or corrective/preventive action:

- *Was the employee sufficiently trained?* No? Train personnel in proper procedures and techniques.

- *Were the proper tools available and used?* No? Obtain and assure the use of the right tools for the job.

- *Do work instructions include sufficient detail and caution notes?* No? Revise the instructions to include understandable detail and caution notes.

- *Is an adequate machine maintenance program in effect and current?* No? Revise your maintenance program so that it not only precludes a recurrence but also provides preventive measures on similar equipment.

- *Was an adequate system available and adhered to?* No? Assure dissemination of information through devices such as "read and initial" memos or regular supervisor shop talks.

Remember, removing the cause of the deficiency reduces the possibility of the deficiency repeating itself. If you don't correct the cause, you cannot correct the problem.

You can't stop the birds from flying over your head
but you can prevent them from
nesting in your hair.

Martin Luther King

Documentation

A properly documented corrective action response will include the essential elements listed as follows:

- The immediate action or "fix."

- Action taken to locate and correct any other parts or material that may contain the same condition.

- Review of system and determination as to the cause of the condition.

- Preventive action to eliminate the cause and preclude recurrence of the condition.

- Establish affectivity of the corrective action by serial number, lot number, or date as applicable.

Followthrough

A corrective action needs to be a continuous commitment. All too often we implement corrective actions like we take antibiotics. We are faithful until the symptoms go away, then we stop or relax because it doesn't appear to be a problem anymore.

As with an antibiotic you need to continue long after the symptoms go away or else the virus or deficiency will come back with a vengeance.

Examples The following examples illustrate both acceptable and unacceptable corrective action. Unfortunately, these are actual examples of unacceptable corrective actions that had to be revised.

Corrective Action 1

Event: Insulator bonded on wrong side of circuit.

Defect: IDD XXX-XXXX-XXX insulator near T2 designation is on front side of board, should be on rear side.

Cause: Work instruction error, engineering change not incorporated.

Not Acceptable:

- Production engineering has been contracted and will revise the instruction, per telecon _____.
- Part has been properly installed.

Acceptable:

- Work instruction for operation 70 will be revised by _____ (production engineer, J. Smith, ext. 1234).
- No other parts now in work.
- Check of stock shows two parts made prior are squawked and submitted to Material Review on Rejection Notice 2345.
- See enclosed Inspection Layout 34567 for corrective action from production engineering and quality engineering.

98

Corrective Action 2

Event: During functional test, a short circuit was detected in a module.

Defect: Connector contacts A51 and A52 are shorted beneath the heat sink. Reference DA/DR 9999.

Cause: Workmanship, operator error.

Not Acceptable:

Unable to ascertain responsible operator; told operators to use extreme care in soldering.

Acceptable:

- Manufacturing supervisor has provided special training and instruction to operators engaged in rail installation, reference training letter #400-9-26, on _____.

- Defect caused by reflowing solder under heat sink.

Corrective Action 3

Event: Work instruction error.

Defect: Work instruction for part number 1234, page 3, calls out $^{11}/_{16}$ inch dimension (0.6875) for component height. Drawing calls out 0.685 maximum.

Cause: Work instruction analyst had rounded off a decimal dimension to the nearest fraction, allowing component lead dimensions to exceed drawing tolerance by 0.0025 inch.

Not Acceptable:

- The work instruction has been revised to agree with the 0.685 inch dimension.

Acceptable:

- The work instruction has been revised to agree with the 0.685 inch limit.

- Responsible personnel in production engineering have been instructed on this type of error to prevent recurrence.

- The specific responsible individual is no longer assigned to this function.

- A check tool has been made available to inspection to verify component installation.
- All parts that have been through the assembly sequence have been rechecked and are within the required dimension.

Corrective Action 4

Event: Supplier failed to process parts to an approved subcontractor.

Defect: Aluminum castings — anodized finish not accomplished by a company-approved source; supplier certification incorrect.

Cause: Supplier had obtained a better cost for anodizing from an outside subcontractor and failed to require finishing by a controlled/approved source.

Not Acceptable:

Future buys will be sent to approved anodize finishers only.

Acceptable:

- Supplier reviewed the internal subcontract controls and found that no system existed for review of finish requirements.
- A quality planning checkpoint has been added to all future subcontract orders to assure issuance to qualified/approved sources only.

Corrective Action 5

Event: Drilling error.

Defect: Five mislocated holes on one part.

Cause: The mechanic inadvertently used the wrong dimensions during layout of the hole location.

Not Acceptable:

Mechanic was notified of the defects and was cautioned.

Acceptable:

- The mechanic was advised of his or her layout error.
- A hole location template was manufactured, eliminating the need for future layout of the holes.
- The operation sheet has been revised to require use of this template.
- Similar layout operations are being analyzed to determine the need for templates.

Similar Items or Products Based on the above investigation, one should analyze similar products that could also have a similar deficiency. All too often we are myopic in our corrective action processes.

Pay me now or pay me later.

FOLLOW-UP AUDITS

The need for a follow-up audit should be seriously reviewed. This is another disruption to the auditee; therefore, only the more serious deficiencies should be physically evaluated. It is preferable if a supplier sends objective evidence that corrections have been made. This may eliminate the need for a trip. There is a correlation between a needless trip and a doctor who sets up another appointment for something that could be reviewed by telephone.

During the next normally scheduled audit, I have the opportunity to select a corrective action or two and review their continued effectiveness. Often this is the more meaningful follow-up, as it tells you if the corrective action was sufficient to have a lasting effect.

CHAPTER 9

THE PROFESSIONAL'S CHARACTER TRAITS

Progressive quality professionals, meeting the needs of world-class companies, have uncommon personality traits. They are serious about their work because they know it is a significant "drop in the bucket," a positive drop or a negative drop.

- One little drop of water falling into a container of acid may cause an explosion.

- One drop of germ culture introduced into a container of milk can make the liquid dangerous to drink.

- One drop of cleansing disinfectant can neutralize a whole bucket of contaminated water.

The "drop in a bucket" can make a tremendous difference. The focus is on continuous improvement that changes the status quo. For this reason the progressive quality professional needs to be an intelligent diplomat, as change is not a popular activity.

The physician's office library has the requirements and standards to which the patient must comply (purchase orders, law, safety, specification, contracts, and so on) and a file cabinet that provides insight into the patient's history. The patient's current condition is best evaluated by comparing it to the requirements with particular evaluations tailored to the patient through his or her history.

As with any doctor's office, the quality professional uses current inventory (weight) as an indicator. Excessive inventory as well as other maladies identified during the examination of trends form a basis for further examinations. A fishbone diagram (cause-and-effect analysis) is one of the tools used to focus on a more detailed examination. The quality professional also has a pharmacy stocked with other prescriptions (SPC, QFD, Cpk, DOE, CE, PDCA, and so on) that could help in problem solving and health protection.

The purpose of this comparison is to depict a new breed of quality professionals.

NEW BREED OF QUALITY PROFESSIONALS

Great Observers

The quality professional is involved with almost every department of a company and, therefore, has gained a variety of insights. This invaluable background allows the person to perceive quality opportunities by observing an operation and analyzing trends/data.

> *You can see a lot by just observing.*
>
> *Yogi Berra*

Trustworthy

I would not appreciate a doctor who told another patient all about my medical history. Just like doctors, auditors need to treat information confidentially. Violation of this could ruin a company's market share (internal information) or relationship with a supplier (supplier information). This especially is important when a proprietary process is involved.

> *Gossip is the most deadly microbe.*
> *It has neither legs nor wings.*
> *It is composed entirely of tales,*
> *and most of them have stings.*

With the exclusion of proprietary information, both quality and medical professionals take full advantage of their previous experiences. They share this knowledge and experience freely but are very careful to maintain source anonymity when appropriate.

> *Gossip is a highly communicable disease*
> *and leaves people with wicked scars.*

Hard Workers

The people who succeed in their chosen field of endeavor don't necessarily have significantly higher intelligence; they are simply hard workers. Quality, like the medical profession, is not an eight-to-five job; it is a 24-hour-a-day job. I spend a significant amount of time, after hours, reading and studying ways in which my company and I can improve.

Generally speaking,
the great achieve their greatness by industry
rather than by brilliance.

Bruce Barton

Persistent

Quality has never been delivered on a silver platter. A continued drive toward excellence is the key to quality. Just like the Taguchi loss function analysis, we should never be of the opinion that "acceptable" (within upper and lower limits) is cost-effective. We must continually target the optimum as our goal.

Cheerfully Positive

Whether a person is at work, home, or play, he or she listens to a cheerfully positive person more readily than to a negative person. This positive aspect is critical, as any effective communication requires a willing listener. People do not respect those who have a bad attitude. This attitude is not only critical to a person's effectiveness, it is also key to one's promotion.

Promotion awaits the employee who radiates
cheerfulness, not the employee who spreads gloom
and dissatisfaction. Doctors tell us that
cheerfulness is an invaluable aid to health.
Cheerfulness is also an invaluable aid to promotion.

B. C. Forbes

Continuous Improvers

Benchmarking is important, but is overwhelming. Regardless of where you stand in relationship to your competitors, on the top or at the bottom, the true professional is constantly trying to improve.

We should all have lofty goals. When trying to achieve them, we become aware that in life we need to make improvements constantly, even in the little things.

Risk Takers

Achieving improvements will take risk. The professional, while being aware of the risks, is very aware of the failure that belongs to those who do not take risks.

There is one thing that we can count on: All risks are not successful. During my life I have made many mistakes and will probably make several more. Although I regret my mistakes, I also learn from them. The story of a bank president best illustrates how risk-takers mature and succeed.

"What is the secret of your success?" a reporter asked a bank president.

"Two words."

"And what would they be, sir?"

"Right decisions."

"And how do you make the right decisions?"

"Experience."

"And how do you get experience?"

"Two words."

"What are they?"

"Wrong decisions."

A casual look at history will tell you that few of us learn from the mistakes of others; we learn from our own mistakes. As the youngest of four, I did not listen to my older siblings; I made the same mistakes they did and was smart enough to correct my behavior (most of the time).

Unselfish

The quality professional is a catalyst for improved quality. A doctor may help a patient, but it also takes the support staff and the patient's cooperation to make any improvements. We may be the team leader, but as with a doctor or a quarterback, team leaders without a team are only "voices crying in a wilderness."

We need to focus on improvement and give the credit to the department, supplier, or person who achieves the improvement. The true quality professionals will not draw attention to themselves.

There is no limit to
what a man can do or where he can go
if
he doesn't mind who gets the credit.

R.W. Woodruff
Founder, Coca-Cola Company

CONCLUSION

Opportunity isnowhere.

(What does this say?)

As we sharpen our technical knowledge and bedside manner, we will read the above as "Opportunity Is Now Here." Those who elect to maintain the status quo will read it as "Opportunity Is Nowhere."

We in the quality profession need to be committed to excellence!

C H A P T E R   10

TERMS AND
DEFINITIONS

The following is a compilation of terms and definitions that may be used within the quality profession.[2] The definitions are as stated in ISO Committee Draft 8402-1 *Quality–Vocabulary,* 1990-12-10 ISO/TC 176/SC1 N93.

Auditee An organization being audited.

Capability Ability to perform designated activities and to achieve results that fulfill specified requirements.

Compatibility The ability of entities to be used together under specific conditions to fulfill relevant requirements.

Concession See *Waiver.*

Conformity The fulfillment of specified requirements.

Contract Review The systematic activities carried out before signing the contract to ensure that requirements for quality are adequately defined, free of ambiguity, documented, and realizable by the supplier.

Corrective Action An action taken to eliminate the causes of an existing nonconformity, defect, or other undesirable situation to prevent recurrence.

Customer The recipient of a product provided by the supplier.

Defect The nonfulfillment of intended usage requirements.

Dependability The collective term used to describe the availability performance and its influencing factors: reliability performance, maintainability performance, and maintenance support performance.

Design Review A formal, documented, comprehensive, and systematic examination of a design to evaluate the design requirements and the capability of the design to meet the requirement for quality and to identify problems and propose solutions.

Deviation Written authorization prior to production or before provision of a service to depart from specified requirements for a specified quantity or for a specified time.

Disposition of Nonconformity The action to be taken to deal with an existing nonconforming entity to resolve the nonconformity.

Entity An object, tangible or intangible, that can be individually described and considered.

Inspection Activities such as measuring, examining, testing, or gauging characteristics of an entity and comparing the results with specified requirements to determine whether conformity is achieved for each of these characteristics.

Interchangeability The ability of an entity to be used in place of another to fulfill the same requirements.

Hold Point A point defined in an appropriate document beyond which an activity must not proceed without the approval of a designated organization or authority.

Management Review A formal quality evaluation by top management of the status and adequacy of the quality system in relation to quality policy and new objectives resulting from changing circumstances.

Nonconformity The nonfulfillment of specified requirements.

Objective Evidence Information that can be verified, based on facts and obtained through observation, measurement, test, or other means.

Observation (Audit) A statement of fact made during an audit and substantiated by objective evidence.

Organization A company, corporation, firm enterprise or association, or institution, or part thereof, whether incorporated or not, public or private, that has its own function(s) and administration.

Preventive Action An action taken to eliminate the causes of a potential nonconformity, defect, or other undesirable situation to prevent occurrence.

Procedure A specified way to perform an activity.

Process A set of interrelated resources and activities that transforms inputs into outputs with the aim of adding value.

Product The result of activities or processes.

Product Liability A generic term used to describe the onus on a producer or others to make restitution for loss related to personal injury, property damage, or other harm caused by a product or service.

Production Permit A written authorization for a product, prior to its production, to depart from originally specified requirement.

Qualification Process The process of demonstrating whether an entity is capable of meeting specified requirements.

Qualification Status The status given to an entity when it has been demonstrated that it is capable of meeting specified requirements.

Quality The totality of characteristics of an entity that bear on its ability to satisfy stated or implied needs.

Quality Assurance All those planned and systematic actions to be implemented and demonstrated to provide adequate confidence that an entity will satisfy given requirements for quality.

Quality Audit A systematic and independent examination to determine whether quality activities and related results comply with planned arrangements and whether these arrangements are implemented effectively and are suitable to achieve objectives.

Quality Audit Observation A statement of fact made during a quality audit and substantiated by objective evidence.

Quality Auditor A person who has the qualification status to perform quality audits.

Quality Control The operational techniques and activities that are used to fulfill requirements for quality.

Quality Document   A document that contains either requirements for quality system elements of products or results of activities such as inspections or quality audits.

Quality Evaluation   A systematic examination of the extent to which an entity is capable of meeting specified requirements.

Quality Improvement   The actions taken to increase the value to the customer by improving the effectiveness and efficiency of processes and activities throughout the quality loop.

Quality Loop   A conceptual model of interacting activities that influence quality at the various stages ranging from the identification of needs to the assessment of whether these needs have been satisfied.

Quality Losses   The losses caused by not realizing the optimum potential of resources in processes and activities.

Quality Management   All activities of the overall management function that determine the quality policy, objectives, and responsibilities and implement them by means such as quality planning, quality control, quality assurance, and quality improvement.

Quality Manual   A document stating the quality policy and describing the quality system of an organization.

Quality Plan   A document setting out the specific quality practices, resources, and sequence of activities relevant to a particular product, project, or contract.

Quality Planning   Establishing and developing the objectives and requirements for quality and the requirements for the quality system application.

Quality Policy   The overall quality intentions and direction of an organization as regards quality, as formally expressed by top management.

Quality-Related Costs   A part of the overall costs considering the expenses incurred in ensuring and assuring satisfactory quality as well as the tangible and intangible losses incurred when satisfactory quality is not achieved.

Quality Surveillance   The continuous monitoring and verification of the status of procedures, methods, conditions, processes, products, and services and analysis of records in relation to stated references to ensure that specified requirements for quality are being met.

Quality System   The organizational structure, responsibilities, procedures, processes, and resources for implementing quality management.

Quality System Review   A formal evaluation by top management of the status and adequacy of the quality system in relation to quality policy and new objectives resulting from changing circumstances.

Record   A document that furnishes objective evidence of activities performed or of results achieved.

Reliability   The ability of an item to perform a required function under stated conditions for a stated period of time. Also used as a reliability characteristic denoting a probability of success or a success ratio.

Repair   The action taken on a nonconforming item so that it will fulfill the intended usage requirements, although it may not conform to the originally specified requirements.

Rework   The action taken on a nonconforming item so that it will fulfill the originally specified requirements.

Safety   The state in which the risk of harm or damage is limited to an acceptable level.

Self-Inspection   Inspection of the work performed by the performer of that work according to specified rules.

Service   The results generated by activities at the interface between the supplier and the customer and by supplier internal activities to meet customer needs.

Service Delivery   Those supplier activities necessary to provide the service.

Specification   A document stating requirements.

Subcontractor   The organization that provides a product to the supplier.

Supplier The organization that provides a product to the customer.

Total Quality Management A management approach of an organization centered on quality, based on the participation of all its members, and aiming at long-term profitability through customer satisfaction, including benefits to the members of the organization and to society.

Traceability The ability to trace the history, application, or location of an entity by means of recorded identification.

Validation Confirmation by examination and provision of objective evidence that the particular requirements for a specific intended use are met.

Verification Confirmation by examination and provision of objective evidence that specified requirements have been met.

Waiver Written authorization to use or release a quantity of material, components, or stores already produced but that does not conform to the specified requirements.

REFERENCES

1. Imai, Masaaki. *KAIZEN, The Key to Japan's Competitive Success.* New York: Random House, 1986.

2. ISO/CD 8402-1 *Quality—Vocabulary,* 1990-12-10 ISO/TC 176/SC1 N93. Washington, DC: International Standards Organization.

INDEX

Acceptable quality level (AQL), 65
Aerospace Industry Association, 48
Affinity diagram, 65
Allied Quality Assurance Publications (AQAP), 5
American Medical Association (AMA), comparison of ASQC to, 1-2
American National Standards, 4
American Society for Quality Control (ASQC), 1
 code of ethics of, 2-3
 comparison of, to AMA, 1-2
Angell, James Burrill, 50
ANSI/ASQC standards, 4
Arrow diagram, 66
Attitude, of quality professional, 105
Audit
 and early notification, 88-89
 follow-up, 101
 frequency of, 88
 information needed for, 90-91
 performing, 93
 preparing for, 89
 purpose of, 89, 90
 schedule for, 90
 written report of, 94
Auditee, emphathy for, 14-15
Audit worksheets
 customizing, 91-92
 types of, 92
Average (X) and range (R) chart, 86

Loss function
    concept of, 76, 77
    continuous, 76
    Taguchi analysis of, 85

Management, 62
    audit for change in, 20
Management by objective (MBO), 80
Management by wandering around (MBWA), 26, 76, 78
Management for quality
    cooperative strategies, 28-29
    executive strategies, 28
    monitoring effectiveness, 29
    supportive strategies, 29
Maslow, A. H., $37n$
Maturity of product/company, relationship to inventory, 58
Metrics, 38
Motorola, 19, 49

National Institute of Standards and Technology, 69

Observation skills, for quality professional, 104
Operational services, measurement of, 48

Pareto chart, 78
Pareto diagram, 79
Pareto's law, 78
Performance measurement, and employee recognition, 37-38
Persistence, of quality professional, 105
Plan-Do-Check-Act (PDCA), 78-80
Plateau histogram, 74, 75
Poka-yoke, 80
    stages of, 80
Policy deployment (PD), 80
    steps in, 80
PPM defective, 49
Process capability
    continuous improvement of, 41-42
    and quality control, 40-41

Support services
        business process and quality of, 43-44
        measurement of, 48

Taguchi, Genichi, 23
Taguchi loss function analysis, 85
Teamwork, and quality professional, 107
Thomas Group Inc., 69
3M, 19
Throughput, 59
Tooling, 61
Total preventive maintenance (TPM), 86
Total quality companies, 23
Total quality management (TQM), 71, 86
Training. *See* Education
Trends, company, 61
Truncated histogram, 74, 75
Vital few and trivial many principle, 78

Waste process and disposal, 61
Worker attitude surveys, 76
Work ethic, of quality professional, 105
World-class company, 23

X and R chart, 86
Xerox, 19, 49